LOVED & FORGIVEN

**A Bible Commentary for Laymen/Colossians
BY LLOYD JOHN OGILVIE**

Regal
Books
Ventura, CA U.S.A

Dedicated to my mother.

Other good reading in this series:
Liberated for Life (Galatians) by John F. MacArthur, Jr.
Let's Get Moving (Ephesians) by Stuart Briscoe
Pass It On (1 & 2 Timothy) by Robert Mounce
Highlights of the Bible (New Testament) by William L. Lane

The foreign language publishing of all Regal books is under the direction of GLINT. GLINT provides financial and technical help for the adaptation, translation and publishing of books for millions of people worldwide. For information regarding translation, contact: GLINT, P.O. Box 6688, Ventura, California 93006.

A Gospel Light Teacher's Manual and Student Discovery Guide for Bible study groups using *Loved and Forgiven* are available from your church supplier.

The Scripture quotations in this publication, unless otherwise indicated, are from *The New International Version*, New Testament. Copyright © 1973 by New York Bible Society International. Used by permission.

Other Bible versions used:
KJV—Authorized King James Version.
TLB—The Living Bible, Copyright © 1971 by Tyndale House Publishers, Wheaton, Illinois. Used by permission.

Eleventh Printing, 1982

Published by Regal Books
A Division of GL Publications
Ventura, California 93006
Printed in U.S.A.

Library of Congress Catalog Card No. 76-29889
ISBN 0-8307-0442-6

Contents

+ + +

Preface
✛ ✛ ✛

One Sunday morning, after I had preached on a portion of Colossians, a couple made a very unique but gratifying comment. The twinkle in their eyes and their warm laughter communicated affirmation.

"All right, Pastor, there's no way you could have known about us and our needs this past week unless you had bugged our house. You talked this morning like you had overheard every conversation in every room. What you said was just what we needed to hear. We felt like we were the only people in the sanctuary and that you had written your sermon for us."

The miracle of communication had taken place. The experience of the week had focused the couple's hearts on their deepest needs and the Holy Spirit had used the exposition of God's Word to heal and liberate them. The Word of God had spoken to their condition. Their comment made me all the more resolute to be a biblical preacher.

I often feel like that couple when I read and study Colossians. I have the sense that the Apostle has walked in my shoes on the streets of my city. It is timeless and so contemporary. The same problems which confronted the Colossian Christians are still around: beguiling philosophies, distracting addenda to the gospel, competing saviours, polarized asceticism and license, diminutive gods of cultural religion, and insecure Christians unsure of the gospel and equivocating about Christ.

Colossians was written by Paul during his first imprisonment in Rome. Colosse was a Phrygian city in the province of Asia Minor. It was the hotbed of Gnostic philosophic sophistry. The intellectual, spiritual and moral problems, which were faced by the new Christians in the church established there by Epaphras, had a death grip on the future of the fellowship. Epaphras had come to Rome to share their confusion with the great Apostle. Paul's response is one of the most powerful statements of the supreme and sublime adequacy of Christ we have.

My preparation for writing this book was in four stages. I first used it as my scriptural devotional guide. Knowing that nothing can be communicated *through* us until it has been communicated *to* us, I read portions of Colossians each day and allowed them to meet my own needs.

At that time my wife was facing a period of serious illness. Each day Paul led me back to the Saviour and the plentitude of His power. Often I felt that Paul had written the epistle personally for me. In a way he did. I believe that the Scriptures are the inspired Word of God and therefore I am convinced He knew that what He guided Paul to write to the Colossians would also be His special Word to us, centuries later.

The second stage of preparation was to attempt my own translation of the original Greek text. I hope the results of that have seasoned the insights I want to share. I have included several references to the Greek when I thought it would be both helpful and stimulating.

Next, I preached Colossians to my Hollywood congregation, receiving not only a warm response, but a litmus test of what would be most creative to include in this writing.

Lastly, I divided the epistle into 12 sections and wrote what I felt was the particular message for our time. I kept the real people of my city and the ancient city of Colosse in my mind's eye throughout.

Each chapter seeks to accomplish both a verse by verse exposition and a development of a central theme. Chapter 1 is the longest because it is an effort to raise the major themes of the epistle, provide introductory background and introduce us to the perplexed and floundering Christians in Colosse whom Paul tried to reestablish in the triumphant sufficiency of Christ. In each chapter I have tried to identify the similarity of the Colossians' problems with our own, and thus to write in a personal way about how we can discover the fullness of Christ for the emptiness in us and our world.

Christ is all we need. That's the burning conviction of my life and ministry. In Him we find the fullness of God and the fullness of our potential. My prayer is that through this study the fullness in Christ which Paul offered the Colossians will be ours in a greater and more victorious way.

The New International Version, New Testament is the translation used except where noted. I am thankful for the faithful help of my assistant, Norma Soll; secretary, Esther Bowen; and typist, Gloria Glass, in the preparation of the manuscript.

Getting Our Heads Straight

+ + +

Colossians 1:1-18

The questions will not go away. They lurk beneath the surface like a restless cellar gang that raps with importunity on the basement ceiling of our minds. At times of personal or social problems, they break free from their carefully constructed compartments of evasion and stalk through the corridors of our minds. Tragedy, a renewed realization of the pathos of existence, and confrontation with suffering make putting them off impossible. There will be no peace until they are answered. They shriek in our minds like a demanding inquisition.

How can we believe in a good God in an evil world like this?

How can we explain evil if God is all-loving? Either He knows and does not care, or He cares and can do nothing to help us.

If God is all-powerful, why doesn't He intervene to banish sin, destroy evil, and abort new births of suffering everywhere?

If Christ died for the sins of the whole world, why is there still sin in the world? If the world is still in trouble after 2000 years, what makes us so sure that He is the only way to God? Perhaps He's one way among others.

Questions like these demand that we "get our heads straight." This contemporary expression is used to suggest that there are times when the pressures of life, the difficulty of relationships, and the problems all around us get to us and we need to retreat for a time of hard thinking. It implies that messy thinking results in a muddled life.

Confusion in our hearts about life is the outcome of conflict in our heads. As a noted theologian said, "There is nothing on my heart that has not first been in my head." He was right! Turbulent emotions, immobilized wills, and tension-infected bodies are the result of fuzzy thinking. There has seldom been a time more than now when clear thinking has been needed about Christ, the cross, and the implications of the gospel for the tough issues of life.

The Christians in the infant Colossian church faced the same questions we face. Distorted answers almost destroyed the church. Paul's letter to the Colossians was an effort to help them get their heads straight. Epaphras, who had founded the church for Paul while the Apostle was in Ephesus, had come to Rome for help. His people were in trouble. Though in chains awaiting trial, Paul received him joyfully and listened intently to his account of the difficulties in the Colossian church.

Colosse was situated on the Lycus River, a tributary of the Meander, about a hundred miles from Ephesus and about 12 miles beyond Laodicea. It was not an important town in the province of Asia, but the problems of the church there gave motivation for the most complete and comprehensive statement by Paul of the unique and supreme adequacy of Christ. As Bishop Lightfoot says in his *Commentary on St. Paul's Epistle to the Colossians and Philemon,* "The doctrine of the Person of Christ is here stated with greater precision and fulness than in any other of Paul's epistles."[1] And for good reason.

A virulent poison had infected the lifeblood of the church. Gnosticism was rampant in Colosse, inflicting intellectual and philosophic conflict and an erosion of assurance among the Christians.

The Gnostics had gained their name from the Greek word *gnosis,* meaning "knowledge." They claimed a superior and esoteric knowledge in answer to some of the basic questions of life we still face today.

How was the world created?

How can evil by explained?

How could an absolute God create a world in which evil exists?

Either God created evil or He is completely aloof from His creation.

A carefully structured philosophic school of thought developed in an effort to explain the questions. The Gnostics asserted that God was distantly separated from the world. Creation had taken place as a result of a series of emanations. Each was more distant from God, until those furthest from Him created the material world. The reasoning went something like this: matter was evil, spirit was good; God was a spirit and therefore good; the material world was evil and thus could not have contact with a spiritual God; He created the world through issuing emanations; these were separate and often antagonistic to Him.

A simplistic theory of life, indeed, but one that had grave influence on the infant church. The Christians believed that God had come in the flesh in Jesus Christ to love, forgive, and reconcile the world. The Incarnation became the center of conflict. The Gnostics expressed the sophistry of their reasoning. They began with a fallacious assumption and reasoned to a distorted end.

Starting again with the idea that matter was evil, they argued that flesh was evil. If Jesus was the Son of God, He could not have dwelt in the flesh. He must have been little more than one of the many emanations from God; at most, one of a gradation of angels. Follow that to its conclusion and you can understand why they said that Jesus did not live as a man, He did not suffer on the cross, and He did not rise from the dead because He had never lived in an evil, material body.

Some Gnostics conceded the uniqueness of Christ, but held tenaciously to the dichotomy of good and evil, spirit and matter, saying that the Spirit hovered over Jesus only from the time of His baptism and left before His crucifixion. No wonder the Christians in Colosse were in trouble! The gospel they had received from Epaphras was under attack.

The inroads into the church came from a group called the Essenes, a mystic and ascetic brotherhood of very exclusive Jews. They prided themselves in secret religious doctrines known only to the initiated few. Their intellectual framework was Gnostic, but their religious practices were based on a fanatic extension of Mosaic legalism.

The Essenes' asceticism went to extremes. They held marriage, eating animal flesh, affirmation of the body, and enjoyment of life in equal disdain. Their rigorous observance of rites and rituals was compulsive. Adding to the Mosaic tradition, they worshiped the sun, an elaborate gradation of angels, and their own system of religious secrets.

The Essenes' harassment of the church was focused not only in the infiltration of Gnostic ideas, but in an unsettling demand that the Christians fulfill the regulations and requirements of their distorted brand of Mosaic Judaism.

This background helps us to understand the meaning behind what Paul wrote to Colosse. Any penetrating exposition of the epistle must move on three levels: what Paul said and why he said it; what it meant to the Colossians; and what it now means to us as we seek to answer the profound questions of life.

In Colossians 1:1-18 there are seven crucial antidotes for the anxiety caused by the confused thinking which had infected the church. Paul wanted the struggling Christians to know who they were by God's grace; to Whom they belonged; what had been

11

done for them; the unlimited power available to them; and what the gospel had to say about the complex issues of good and evil gripping the intellectual and religious life of their city.

The theme which is woven through this first section of the letter is that Christ is God's answer to the problem of evil and that He has called a new breed of humanity, the Church, to be the demonstration of His intention for all mankind. Every word is carefully chosen to paint a liberating new self-image for Christians. The assurances become seven challenging admonitions.

Affirm Who You Are

The source of Paul's affirmation of the Colossian Christians was rooted in his own confidence in Christ. His salutation begins with a bold identification of his calling: "Paul, an apostle of Christ Jesus by the will of God" (Col. 1:1). He was a prisoner in Rome, and yet he thought of himself not as an incarcerated criminal hopelessly awaiting the fate of his trial, but as a messenger of Christ, chosen by God, an apostle with divine appointment.

We wonder if Paul savored the words, reflecting on what he had been and what Christ had enabled him to become. Chapters of autobiography are compressed into this one statement. The rigid, compulsive Pharisee of Tarsus had been liberated from self-justifying religion to become the contagious communicator of new life in Christ. This seasoned adventurer of the Lord had known excruciating persecution, rejection, hardship and danger, but in it all he had known an unquenchable, artesian joy. That enthusiasm for Christ and His calling galvanized the fellowship of the Christians with him in Rome. They knew they were a part of Christ's movement to change the world.

This supportive fellowship is indicated by Paul's reference to "Timothy our brother." How very gracious! His "son in the faith" (1 Tim. 1:2) was now his brother in the Lord. I think he acted as Paul's scribe for the Colossian letter. Imagine the joy that filled Timothy's heart and the smile that broadened across his face as he wrote down these words.

Timothy had come a long way from the first time he had heard the courageous Apostle speak in his home town of Lystra, east of Colosse. He had watched as Paul was stoned by the angry mob. He was probably an onlooker as the faithful disciples gathered around Paul to pray for his healing. As a young man, Timothy saw a vivid example of what Christ could do in a person. He was ready when Paul returned later and enlisted him as one of his missionary band.

Now as he wrote Paul's dictated greeting to the troubled Christians at Colosse, Timothy felt the Apostle's love for them. They were feeling defeated and unfaithful, and yet Paul did not remind them of their failures, but of their faithfulness. The greeting was consistent with the Apostle's gift of encouragement. Surely Timothy felt joy pulsate through him as he formed the words with his reed pen.

"To the holy and faithful brothers in Christ at Colosse" (Col. 1:2). What a dynamic designation for discouraged people! Paul knew that they could not survive in the intellectual confusion and philosophic ambiguity of Colosse if they were not also in Christ. Some of them were weakening and were shaken in their allegiance to Christ. Others were dabbling in subtle synthesis of the gospel with distorting Gnostic ideas rampant throughout their city. Yet, Paul calls them faithful Christian brothers. He knew that they didn't need to be reminded of how bad they were, but of how great their God was.

The *King James Version* translates the salutation, "To the saints and faithful brethren in Christ." The word saint is drenched with meaning. Paul used the term in his epistles as a sublime synonym for Christ's people. The Greek word, *hagios*, means "a holy person." Holy designates what belongs to God. Here the term identifies a person who is set apart: God's person, called and appointed to live for Him; devoted, consecrated, separated. Paul believed that the Colossian Christians had been elected to salvation by grace and the process of sanctification—growing in holiness—was at work in them. Their sainthood was a gift of God. He had loved, forgiven, called, indwelt and empowered them.

The companion word "faithful," which Paul uses, expresses his confidence in the troubled believers. The designation many of them probably felt they deserved the least, helped them remember who they were in spite of their problems.

We will miss the full impact of our study of Colossians unless we can read this opening affirmation inserting our own name and church. We are God's saints regardless of our performance or adequacy. Nothing can change that settled truth. We have been called, appointed, valued, cherished and loved by the

Lord. He came, lived, died and was raised up for us. His Spirit has been at work in us, convincing us of His love and giving us the gift of faith to respond. It is with awe and wonder that we acknowledge our status as saints of God.

But status without strength to live the new life in Christ results in frustration. If we are to make it in our contemporary Colosse, we need the reality of the greeting Paul wrote the Colossians: "Grace and peace to you from God our Father" (1:2). Grace explains God's nature and attitude toward us and peace is what happens in us when we accept His love and forgiveness through His Son.

The Greek word for grace is *charis*, "freely given love." Christ and His cross focus God's unmerited love. We cannot earn it or ever deserve it. We can never be good enough. Grace is unmotivated love. There is nothing we are or have done which motivates God to love us. He loves us because He is love.

If the Christian life does not begin with an experience of grace it has no real beginning; but if it begins with grace there is no end to its growth and adventure. The grace of God melts our cold self-assertiveness and astounds us with the realization that we are loved in spite of what we have been and done. That's what happened to John Newton when unchanging love broke into his wild, vagabond life. After years of rebellion, he was captured by grace:

In evil long I took delight,
Unawed by shame and fear,
Till a new object struck my sight,
And stopped my wild career.
Amazing grace! how sweet the sound,

That saved a wretch like me!
I once was lost, but now I'm found,
Was blind, but now I see.

Paul wanted to remind the Colossians that God was not aloof from His creation. Grace was the instigation of the Incarnation. Sheer grace was revealed in the life and death of Christ. Unlimited grace was available to the saints for daily pressures and frustrations. The victory of Christ over the forces of evil was the victory they could know. They were not helpless victims of powers beyond their control. They were under the control of the grace of God.

Peace results from grace. The word *eirene* means "binding together," the unification of what is broken and fragmented. For Paul, peace was inseparable from the cross. We have peace with God through the blood of the cross. There is no peace until we know we are loved, forgiven, and accepted. That peace enables us to accept ourselves and others. The warfare inside us is over and we can become peacemakers in the conflict around us. Self-incrimination and negation are finished when we accept Christ's death on the cross as our only hope. Penetrating peace pervades our minds and hearts. It is the undeniable inner assurance that we have experienced the grace of God. We need to get our heads straight about that!

Accept What God Has Done

Paul wanted the Colossians to be confident of what God had done in their lives. It was one thing to tell them that they were the saints of God, but they needed to be sure. Under the pressure of the challenges of the Gnostics and the Essenes, the temptation to doubt what had happened to them was very disturbing.

The Apostle confirms their changed lives in a very winsome way. He tells them about his prayers for them. The gathered church in Paul's quarters in Rome had been praying about them. Think of what that must have meant to the struggling Christians! Paul and his friends not only knew of their difficulties, they were aware of the evidences of Christ at work in their lives. "We always thank God, the Father of our Lord Jesus Christ, when we pray for you, because we have heard of your faith in Christ Jesus and of the love you have for all the saints" (1:3,4). What delight that must have infused into the hearts of the Colossians! Their faith in Christ and the love He gave them for each other was not a wish-dream.

But Paul longed for them to understand clearly that what had happened to them was because of the gospel. He rooted them in the objective truth. The good news of Christ's life and death for them was the source and substance of their new freedom and joy. The seed of truth had been planted in them and was springing up in the quality of their lives: "The faith and love that spring from the hope stored up for you in heaven, and which you have already heard about in the word of truth, the gospel that has come to you" (1:5,6).

We all need to be sure of that. We need to get our heads straight about the gospel. Our faith is not dependent on our feelings but on what God has done in Christ. The reorienting truth liberates us. We return to the cross constantly to rediscover the truth about our condition and God's compassion. A cosmic reconciliation has been accomplished for us. Death's power has been defeated. We are alive in Christ now and forever. Hope flows from this knowledge in limitless supply, stored up for us in heaven. In the light of the gospel, we can grapple with the perplexing questions about the power of evil and the sick and suffering world around us. What has happened to us through the gospel is God's answer to the riddle of evil. What He did in Christ defeats the power of evil for those who believe in Him.

And we are not alone. The Lord is on the move changing lives all over the world. The Colossians needed to know that they were part of the dynamic movement of God. That's why Paul assured them that the same gospel which had changed their lives was changing men and women wherever its power was proclaimed: "All over the world this gospel is producing fruit and growing, just as it has been doing among you since the day you heard it and understood God's grace in all its truth" (1:6).

The Greek suggests that the good-news seed was inherently reproductive. The germination and growth came from the inherent energy in the seed. Once planted in the receptive mind and willing heart, it would spring up and grow to maturity. Note that Paul says that hearing and understanding God's grace in all its truth is the key. Epaphras had scattered the seed; the Colossians had provided the fertile soil.

By sharing the prayers of thanksgiving of the church at Rome for the church at Colosse, Paul had wanted to establish some very powerful truths. The Colossians need not feel insecure in their faith. They

18

were bearing the fruit of the gospel. The Spirit, the living Christ in their hearts, was the limitless, undiminishable resource of their new life. They were in the mainstream of what the Lord was doing all over the world. He would not change His attitude toward them. Their new life was built on the sure foundation of the truth of the gospel and the experience of Christ Himself.

Ask for the Knowledge of His Will

Next, Paul shares the content of his prayers of intercession: "For this reason, since the day we heard about you, we have not stopped praying for you and asking God to fill you with the knowledge of his will through all spiritual wisdom and understanding" (1: 9).

There are three crucial words in this sentence, all of which were used by the proud Gnostics. They pretended to have a superior possession of them. Paul asserts that they are available only as a gift from God given to the Christians. The Greek word for knowledge used here is *epignosis*, a deeper, broader, and more complete knowledge. For the Gnostic, this knowledge was the result of his effort to understand; for the Christian, knowledge of God was the result of God's self-revelation in Christ.

But the person in Christ had something more. The second word Paul uses is wisdom, *sophia*, the whole composite of mental faculties. In 1 Corinthians 12, Paul identifies wisdom as a gift of the Holy Spirit. The indwelling Spirit provides a capacity to know the very nature of God and His will for all situations. James 1:5,6 affirms this. "If any of you lacks wisdom, he should ask God, who gives generously to all without finding fault, and it will be given to him. But when he asks, he must believe and not doubt, because he who doubts is like a wave of the sea, blown and tossed by the wind." The Lord will give us incisive sagacity beyond our intellectual capabilities. His Spirit infuses insight in our minds into the mysteries of God's plan and purpose, and discernment into what we are to be and do.

Further, the Colossians could claim the implication of knowledge and wisdom in the gift of understanding. The word is *sunesis*, the very wonderful gift of insight which can discriminate between what is true and false. One with this gift can comprehend the relationship of one thing to another, enabling supernatural reasoning ability.

Paul is saying that the Colossian Christians need not be afraid. If the philosophers and religionists who tried to rattle them claimed special capacities known only to them, the Christian had gifts from God in superlative degree.

The same gifts are offered to us. Our intellectual life can be profound because God's Spirit implants thoughts and truths for our answers to life's complexities and questions.

The main thing Paul wanted the Colossians to know through his prayers of intercession was that they could know God's will. The Christian life is not an aimless drifting in a sea of uncontrollable eventualities. A person in Christ can have implanted in him the mind of the Saviour. But discovering the will of the Lord is not a chance insight; it is the result of consistent communion. The unique quality of the new people in Christ is that they can have guidance for all of life's decisions and challenges. But that spells responsibility. Guidance is not for the collection of ideas, but for the living of a life which reproduces the Saviour's character. It is to that challenge that Paul presses on.

Assume Accountability for the Way You Live

Intercession for the Colossians now flows into supplication: "And we pray this in order that you may live a life worthy of the Lord and may please him in every way; bearing fruit in every good work, growing in the knowledge of God" (Col. 1:10). A very vivid image is used by the Apostle. The words picture a scale. What Christ has done and is doing for the Christians is on one side; the Christians' behavior and conduct is on the other. To live a life worthy of the Lord means having weight which balances the weight of the Lord's love at the other side of the scale. The word *axios* means "weighing as much as another thing."

The authentic motive of living the Christian life is the love of Christ for us. He has made his home in us in order to express His love and forgiveness through us. We have been empowered to do what He did and to be to others what He has been to us. Our relationship with Him is not an end in itself. It must result in attitude and action. We do not live a life worthy of the Lord in order to earn His love but because of the love we have received already.

Of course, the imagery is not adequate: We can never balance the scales—the Lord's love always exceeds ours. But we want to please Him because we know that His pleasure in us will never end.

The bearing of fruit is always inadvertent. There can be no fruit without the planting of the seed and the growth of the plant. Root and fruit are inseparable. The more we focus on Christ, the more we become like Him. When He gave us the secret of victorious living He used the image of the vine and the branches, "Apart from me you can do nothing" (John 15:5). Apart from Christ there are no Christian ethics or responsible behavior. When our lives are inconsistent with Him, we will be in constant difficulty and frustration. Most of our troubles, and our frantic reaction to them, are caused by an effort to produce fruit without the sustenance of the vine. We would never expect a branch to produce grapes if we had cut it off from the vine.

Appropriate the Strength He Offers

Paul now explains that strength comes to us from the vine. His prayer of further supplication is that the Colossians would be "strengthened with all power according to his glorious might so that you may have great endurance and patience, and joyfully giving thanks to the Father" (Col. 1:11,12). This is one of my favorite verses in the New Testament. I have repeated it at times of trial and challenge. It helps me to remember that my fatigue, inadequacy, and limitation can be replaced with the power of the Holy Spirit. When I feel empty and done-in because I have come to the end of my resources, I now can thank God because I know that it is in a time like this that I receive the energizing strength of the Spirit. My prayer is that I will realize the inexhaustibility of the

Lord all of the time, not just when I am at the end of my tether. And it's happening. What Paul prayed for the Colossians has become the indefatigable reservoir for me.

To be strengthened with all power means "empowered with all power"—enabling power—uplifting, engendering, energizing. The reason for this is that the power we experience is from the "glorious might" of God Himself. The liberating secret of triumphant living is that we were never meant to have adequate resources to do God's work on our own. It's ludicrous to try. We cannot love, forgive, care, nor make a difference in people's lives and our world on our own strength. Power is given to do those things we could never do alone.

The reason I lived for so long without realizing the power of the Holy Spirit is that I was attempting only those things which I could do easily on my own strength. One day a friend asked me what I was daring to do that only God's power could accomplish. I was alarmed to discover that my life was limited, cautious, and fearful.

The adventure of Christianity began when I moved beyond self-reliance to dare to attempt those guided impossibilities that only the Lord could achieve. It was then that I knew what Paul meant by "glorious might." The Greek word is *kratos*, meaning "perfect strength." It is glorious in that it belongs to God, is a manifestation of His Spirit, and is intended to bring honor to Him, not to me as the channel.

There are three great gifts which are ours when we are empowered with all-power: endurance, patience, and joy. We need all three as much as the Colossians did. The order in the Greek text puts patience first. A.T. Robertson in his *Word Pictures in the New Testament*[2] helped me to understand that patience as it is used here relates to perseverance, a brave patience, with which the Christian contends against various hindrances, persecutions, and temptations which confront him. The word *hupomone*, "patience," means to remain under difficulties empowered by the situational strength of the Holy Spirit.

Endurance, or long-suffering as it is translated in some versions, means patience applied to relationships with people. The Spirit enables a capacity to relate to people with the long endurance of God. Endurance does not retaliate, is not easily provoked to spiteful anger, and endures rejection and injury. Both endurance and patience result from an experience of God's gracious love. When we realize what He has forgiven in us, we can forgive; when we are able to see people and situations from His perspective, we can trust Him, and love people as they are and in spite of what they do.

The outward manifestation of this inner grace is joy. Joy, *chara*, flows from grace, *charis*. When we know that we are loved and cherished by God, joy floods our emotions. It is far superior to happiness which is dependent on circumstances and people. Joy is love growing in the soil of difficulties and suffering. In Galatians 5:22, Paul identifies joy as a fruit of the Spirit. A disposition under the control of the indwelling Spirit is filled with joy. The sure sign that the living God has taken up residence in us is that joy is the consistent attitude of our lives in spite of what we are enduring with patience. It is more than a gushy, flippant exuberance. Rather, joy is the ecstasy of being loved by God which shines in our countenance and sparkles in our character.

Abound in the Settled Security
of the New Creation

Paul's mind now leaps to the new creation. A new age, a new beginning for all creation, has begun because of the death and resurrection of Jesus Christ.

The idea behind these next three verses (Col. 1:12-14) is based on the radial transition of a whole nation of defeated people to a new land. The Apostle took a known to communicate an unknown. The Hebrew people in the Northern Kingdom had been taken to Assyria just as the people in the Southern Kingdom were exiled in Babylon. This was a common practice in the ancient world. Often, after liberation and release, the nation of people was able to return to their homeland.

The imagery Paul used would be familiar history to people in a Roman province. Building on that idea, he wanted the Colossians to abound in the triumphant transfer, through Christ, into the Kingdom of God. Like liberated people, they had been rescued and transferred. Not only that, they were partakers in the inheritance of the people of God. He has "qualified you to share in the inheritance of the saints in the kingdom of light. For he has rescued us from the dominion of darkness and brought us into the kingdom of the Son he loves, in whom we have redemption, the forgiveness of sins" (1:12-14).

The inheritance had four legacies for new life in the new age. *First*, the Colossians were transferred from darkness into light. The truth of the gospel had enabled them to see God as He was, themselves in need of grace, and others as they were. Intellectual light had dawned on their minds. Illumination had penetrated the deep, dark places of their souls. *Second*, the dawn of forgiveness and hope had opened eternity. *Third*, the result was that they were no longer slaves, but free men and women. They had been transferred from slavery to freedom. The word for rescued, *ersato*, means the emancipation of a slave by the purchase and liberation of someone else. *Fourth*, Christ, the emancipator, had set them free of guilt, fear, and sin. They now belonged in His Kingdom. In the realm of His rule there is no longer condemnation, but freedom. Life is not under the domination of the power of Satan and his kingdom of darkness anymore. The challenge is to claim the liberation and live with joyous thanksgiving for what God has done.

Now we have the basis of incisive answers to the questions with which we began this chapter. We can believe in a good God because He has called us out of the possession of the evil world to be His people. What has happened to us is for all people. Our inheritance is to be shared.

The only way to survive in a world like ours is to accept Christ's power over evil and begin to live sustained by His propitious power. Two words signal our hope. Redemption, *apolutrosis*, the "payment of a ransom;" and liberation, *aphesis*, the "release from bondage." These favorite Pauline words unbind us to abound in the new creation in spite of the evil world around us. Then our purpose and passion becomes sharing the hope we have found. Instead of muddling over questions of evil, we become part of God's strategy to transfer all people from bondage to freedom.

Aggregate the Immeasurable Riches of Jesus Christ

Paul's rhetoric now soars to a sweeping crescendo as he tells the Colossians about the supreme adequacy of Jesus Christ. He seems to want to accomplish two things: to show the new Christians that everything he has prayed for on their behalf is available through Christ; and to confront the demeaning of Christ by the Gnostics who refused to accept the Incarnation as the ultimate revelation of God. He uses very dramatic and impelling language to construct his apologetic of the irreplaceable centrality of Christ.

First, Christ is the "image of the invisible God" (1:15). The word "image" is *eikon*. It has several uses that help us plumb the depths of what Paul meant. An eikon was a representation, or reproduction with precise likeness, derived exactly from the prototype. An image of a sovereign or hero on a coin, or a painted portrait of a person's likeness, was an *eikon*. Another example which is helpful is that legal contracts in ancient times not only had a person's signature, but a description of his features and characteristics. This was called an *eikon*.

The word *eikon* also means manifestation, an observable exhibition. What Paul wanted to establish was that Jesus was the exact likeness of God. More than that, He was God Himself in a human incarnation. That cut to the core of the Gnostic equivocation

27

about Christ as one emanation or angel from God. It also exposes the fallacious simplicity of people in our time who say there are many roads to God, that Christ is one way and not the only way.

The Gnostics were on an endless search for and contemplation about the *logos*, the divine Word, wisdom, and reason. *Eikon* is another word for *logos*. The two words are used interchangeably by Philo in *Concerning the Creator of the World*.

The Apostle put his case directly: Christ is the *logos* of God, the *eikon* in whom we meet and comprehend the true nature and character of God, an *eikonion*, an absolutely reliable portrait.

Secondly, Christ is the "firstborn over all creation" (1:15). Christ has priority and sovereignty over creation. "Firstborn" implies honor, favor, chosenness, uniqueness. Psalm 89:27 uses the word for the Messiah: "Also I will make him my firstborn, higher than the kings of the earth" (*KJV*). Paul meant that Christ has more than supremacy over the rulers of the earth. More profoundly, he wanted to convey that Christ was not only uncreated, but was Himself the creator. John catches the majesty of this conviction. "In the beginning was the Word, and the Word was with God, and the Word was God. He was with God in the beginning. Through him all things were made; without him nothing was made that has been made. In him was life, and that life was the light of men" (John 1:1-4).

Christ is Lord of all creation. Paul states it plainly: "For by him all things were created: things in heaven and on earth, visible and invisible, whether thrones or powers or rulers or authorities; all things were created by him and for him" (Col. 1:16). Again Paul reveals a confrontation with the Gnostic system of angels and intermediaries between man and God. Thrones, powers, rulers, and authorities were terms used for the different gradations of angels. Paul sweeps them all away asserting that Christ is not just one of them, but, if they exist at all, they were created by Christ and are under His lordship. Christ is the sole mediator between God and man! "He is before all things, and in him all things hold together" (1:17).

Thirdly, the creator of the world is also the creator of the new humanity, the Church. Having stated the universal supremacy of Christ, Paul now deals with the absolute unity of origin of creation and the Church: "And he is the head of the body, the church; he is the beginning and the firstborn from among the dead, so that in everything he might have the supremacy" (1:18). The Head of the Body, Christ is the mainspring, the unifying guidance, the inspiration of the Church. Life emanates from Him and is sustained by Him. In this verse, "firstborn" has a different meaning in Greek than before. *Arche*, beginning, means "priority of time" and gives "firstborn" more than the idea of pre-existence, as used in verse 15. The firstborn from among the dead means that Christ was the first to rise from the dead. His resurrection was the beginning of the new humanity. As the resurrected Saviour, He reigns as head of the Church.

The imagery grips our minds. In Christ, we are alive in the abundant life, now and forever. The Church is the fellowship of the resurrected people who have been raised to newness of life and liberated from the power of death. The resurrected Lord is supreme leader of the Church as the colony of the resurrection.

All of this has left me deeply stirred and moved. Listening in on the prayers of Paul for the Colossians fills me with praise and thanksgiving. Nothing has been left out. All that we need is offered to us in Christ. If we can comprehend what is ours, we can get our heads straight about life and all its questions. What's in our heads will control what's in our hearts. We turn our attention to that in the next chapter.

Footnotes

1. J.B. Lightfoot, *Commentary on St. Paul's Epistle to the Colossians and Philemon.* (Grand Rapids: Zondervan Publishing House, 1957), p. 120.

2. Archibald Robertson, *Word Pictures in the New Testament.* (Nashville, Tennessee: Broadman Press, 1943), p. 476. This same insight is given by Kenneth S. Wuest in *Word Studies—Ephesians and Colossians.* (Grand Rapids: Wm. B. Eerdmans Publishing Company, 1947), p. 178.

Getting Our Feelings Sorted Out

+ + +

Colossians 1:19-23

There are four deep, undeniable emotional needs we all have in common. We may be packaged differently in the wrapping of a unique individuality, but beneath the trimmings we are all the same on the feeling level. We need to *be loved*, to *feel forgiven*, to *experience security*, and to *sense an adequate hope* for the future. All of our other emotional needs for acceptance, esteem, affirmation, freedom, and purposefulness flow from these basic four.

One of the most alarming realizations of life is that other people cannot satisfy these needs. No one can love us as much as we need to be loved. No person can give us an adequate experience of forgiveness. Security does not come from people or circumstances. Hope must spring from something more than another person's assurance that everything will work out and we should not worry.

Our emotional needs are part of our created nature. God made us that way. We were created for relationship with Him. Only fellowship with God can fill the emptiness of our emotional natures. The gospel is not only truth about God, it is the offer of a new relationship with Him, ourselves, and others which fulfills our emotional needs. It is true that nothing can be in our hearts that has not first been in our heads; but if what's in our thinking does not reach our feelings, we will not be able to live the abundant life Jesus offered. He said that we were to know the truth and the truth would set us free. We not only need to get our heads straight, we need to get our feelings sorted out.

It is on the emotional level that most of us are blocked. Some of us have emotional malnutrition as a result of an inadequate experience of love in our childhood or present families and find it difficult to give what we have not experienced. Others of us have felt rejection or the excruciating pain of broken relationships. Still others are racked with the memory of past failures, the inability to forgive ourselves and try again. And then, all of us at times feel the turbulent emotions of anger, impatience, fear, and frustration. Often we don't know what to do with these feelings. Repression results in depression. Explosion results in confusion. There must be some alternative.

Getting our feelings sorted out is crucial not only for ourselves, but for all the people around us. It's not a simple matter. Only God can do it, and that brings us to the foot of the cross. It is there that the love, forgiveness, security, and hope we so desperately need flow in limitless, unreserved power. Charles Spurgeon once said that "there are some sciences that may be learned by the head, but the science of Christ crucified can only be learned by the heart."

The Power of the Cross

Paul wanted the Colossians to know and experience the power of the cross. In Colossians 1:19-23 he clarifies the cross. He deals with the quadrilateral dimensions of our needs as he shows how what was done on Calvary meets these very needs. We will deal with each of them as we move through the dynamic words and verses of this passage.

Paul began by being sure they understood who died for them. What happened on Calvary was absolutely crucial because of who Christ is. He is the unlimited love of God. In verse 19 of the first chapter Paul makes it undeniably clear: "For God was pleased to have all his fullness dwell in him [Christ]." The Greek words give a meaning which stirs us deeply. *Pleroma*, "fullness," means that with which something is filled. When Paul uses "fullness" in regard to Christ he implies that God's total nature and attributes, powers, and love dwelt in Christ.

In 2 Corinthians 5:19 Paul says: "God was reconciling the world to himself in Christ." Nothing was left out. The fullness of God dwelt in Jesus. And God was pleased to do it because of His love for His creation. He was not forced or coerced. Unmotivated, free, giving grace prompted it. Just as He said: "This is my Son, whom I love; with him I am well-pleased" (Matt. 3:17), at Jesus' baptism, also to you and me He says: "You are my beloved; it is my pleasure to do everything necessary to communicate my love."

The pleasure of God in giving Himself is indicated in Jesus' words: "Do not be afraid, little flock, for your Father has been pleased to give you the kingdom" (Luke 12:32). The cross began in the heart of God. It was His heart's desire to give all of Himself to all of us.

The pleasure of God is to *love* us. He created us as recipients of that delight and esteem-oriented love. He is for us, and we need to know that. Emotional healing and strength come from the knowledge that our Creator loves us and wants to live in fellowship with us. We cannot love ourselves until the love of God waters the dry desert of our souls. Dare to allow yourself to feel that nourishing, encouraging, enabling love. Our excruciating need for love is met by the dynamic love of the cross.

He was pleased to "dwell." That's significant. The Greek word *katoikeo* means to "be at home permanently." *Kata* is "down" and *oikos* is "house" or "home." God was down permanently at home in Christ. It is only through Christ that we know who He was then, and is now. It is not a "transient sojourning" (*paroikeo*), but God's essential being, His very nature which dwelt permanently in Christ. The Word made flesh and now present is God's full, final, ultimate, and essential Word about Himself. That's where the understanding and experience of the cross must begin. Therefore what Christ did is absolutely reliable and trustworthy.

The Cross and Our Failures

That leads us to our second emotional need. We all

34

know failure. We are aware of the things we think, say, and do that separate us from God and people. Sin is just that—separation—whatever blocks our relationship with our loving Lord and the people of our lives. The word sin means to miss the mark like an archer's arrow misses the bull's-eye; to be separated from fellowship with God, for which we were born. Paul goes on now to show us that God's love was given on the cross for our reconciliation. That means forgiveness and a return to a right relationship.

The purpose of God's fullness in Christ was reconciliation. "And through him to reconcile to himself all things, whether things on earth or things in heaven" (Col. 1:20). The judgment and forgiveness of God's love is focused in that statement. Man had rebelled and turned away. Sin is estrangement. It is what we do because we are out of relationship with Him.

Man could not atone for himself. The Jews had tried and ended up with self-justifying pride. Something had to be done. The ransom had to be paid. Ancient Israel had developed the sacrificial system in an effort to atone for its sins. But even that became a tool to evade obedience and a way to manipulate God. There had to be some cosmic atonement enacted in history to reconcile the world.

The word reconciliation used in verse 20 is *apokatallasso*, a combination of *apo*, "back," and *katallasso*, "reconcile"—to bring back to complete harmony and original love in creation. God's attitude to reconciled man is as if man had not sinned and rebelled. An even deeper implication is that, through the blood of the cross, we stand before God as if we had never turned away. The amazing grace is that whenever we claim the forgiveness of the cross, we are put in communion with the very love of God and He relates to us as if there had never been a transgression!

Peace Through the Cross

God, through Christ, reconciled all things to Himself, "by making peace through his blood, shed on the cross" (1:20). The blood of the cross has profound implications for both the Hebrew confusion and the Gnostic controversy in Colosse. Blood was life for the Hebrew. On the day of atonement a lamb was sacrificed on the altar. The shedding of the blood of the lamb was necessary for atonement of sin. Christ, the Lamb of God, gave his lifeblood on the cross. He was the ultimate sacrifice for man's sin.

The blood of the cross was Paul's repudiation of the Gnostic idea that God did not truly dwell in Christ. Some of the Gnostics said that the Spirit came to Jesus at baptism but left before Calvary. Others suggested that the Spirit only hovered over the Saviour. Paul wanted no misunderstanding about what he meant. God dwelt in Christ permanently and died on the cross, His blood shed for all mankind.

John Bunyan put it vividly: "I was made to see, again and again, that God and my soul were friends by his blood; yea, I saw that the justice of God and my sinful soul could embrace and kiss each other through his blood. This was a good day for me; I hope I shall never forget it."

But why? Why was so radical a death necessary? In verse 21, using his readers as an example, Paul explains in a very personal way: "Once you were alienated from God and were enemies in your minds because of your evil behavior."

What the Colossians were like prior to conversion would help them to understand and feel, in an existential way, the plight and pathos of an estranged humanity that made the cross necessary. Paul's explanation of their condition prior to accepting the cross includes all the dimensions of their nature. They were alienated from God; the Greek meaning suggests that they belonged to another. They were estranged from their creator, separated from the Father's love.

The result of their alienation was that they became enemies in mind. Their intellectual capacities were distorted and they worked against God's purpose. Their broken relationship with God had resulted in belligerent emotions. Evil emotions are self-centered, destructive feelings expressed in anger, hatred, jealousy, and demeaning hostility. The result of those kinds of emotions is "evil behavior." The emotion is felt and the deed is performed.

Note the progression: estrangement and separation; confused thinking and misunderstanding; emotional hatred and hostility toward God, self, and others; and finally, actions which express the inner condition. That's the depth of depravity to which man had fallen.

What does that mean to us? Simply that separation from God always results in self-centeredness and pride. How we think results in how we feel; and how we feel dictates what we do. Until we know we are loved and are free to love, we will cause disruption and distortion all around us.

Nothing Can Stop God's Love

Now Paul wants the Colossians to know that they are secure in God's love. Nothing they felt or did could make God stop loving them. Paul's words clap like thunder in our hearts: God "has reconciled [people like those Paul has described] by Christ's physical body through death" (1:22). The word love is not used but it undergirds the whole passage. The constant reminder of what we have been expands the wonder of what God did on the cross. The Colossians had done nothing to deserve that depth of love. Nor have we. When we look back to realize what we have done to life and to the people around us, and then are confronted with the unmerited love of the cross, we are astounded. Our Christian life begins at this point —when we acknowledge our sin and what it cost God.

Now we are ready to experience what the cross means for our security needs. Emotional security results from an indefatigable and unassailable status. We become secure when we experience the stabilizing power of our unchanging standing. God has done that on the cross. The result of that security is emotional maturity. The yo-yo ups and downs of emotional vacillation, the tyranny of changing moods, are over.

We have seen God's response to man's unresponsiveness and now we are ready to feel the power of God's response to responsiveness. Those who accept the love of the cross are given a new status. Paul had used three words to describe all men's condition prior to the cross: We are *alienated, enemies in mind,* and *doing evil deeds.* Now he uses three words to express our condition after accepting the cross. Because of Calvary we are now *holy, without blemish,* and *free from accusation. The Living Bible* paraphrases verse 22 to read: "And now as a result Christ has brought you into the very presence of God, and you are standing there before Him with nothing left against you—nothing left that he could even chide you for."

The word "presence" means to place beside or near. The cross has ushered us out of estrangement into intimate fellowship with God. We are "holy." Our status is one of being consecrated and separated unto God rather than separated from God. We are without blemish. That means that all the blame for our sins has been taken by Christ and suffered for by Him on the cross. *Amomos,* blameless, signifies "without blemish or spot." The word comes from the description of a perfect sacrificial animal. Without blemish also implies ceremonial purification.

The force of the whole idea for us is that because of the cross, God accepts us as cleansed, forgiven, and completely reconciled. Whenever we stand before Him in prayers of confession, He responds with Calvary's love and deals with us as if the sin had not been committed. We are "unaccusable" in His sight —not only cleansed, but exonerated of any charge.

The words "in his sight" are loaded with power. They are a translation of *katenopion* (*kata*— "down"; *en*—"in"; *op*—"to look"). The Lord looks down into our inner souls and sees us as liberated, forgiven people. This knowledge gives us the gift of a new picture of ourselves. We can look down into our own inner being and see what we could become as completely released people.

The Security of the Cross

But there is a provision to this reconciliation. There is a danger that we can fall back into self-justification and self-incrimination. We can stay alive in the cross-oriented experience of love only as we are stablilized in our security. Paul says to "continue in your faith" (1:23), keep focused on the cross. Without the cross we are helpless. The cross communicates the love of God and faith responds.

Never say, "I guess I need more faith!" Faith is not a quantitative commodity. The cross enables faith—calls it forth. We are not to focus on how well or poorly we are living, but on how much God loves us.

The word "continue" in the Greek means "to persist, adhere to, stick with, keep on." To stick to the faith is to say, "Grace solely; Christ only; the cross finally." Then we can sing, "In the cross of Christ I glory," and "Beneath the cross of Jesus I fain would take my stand, a shadow of a mighty rock within a weary land."

That's exactly what Paul means by "established and firm" (v. 23). To stick to the cross means that the house of our lives is built on a sure foundation. Paul wanted the Colossian believers and us to know that we are rooted and grounded on the immovable foundation of Christ. God's love in Christ on the cross was a here and now, once for all, always and forever, rocklike, secure assurance. Paul uses the perfect tense indicating an action in the past, having present results. In Christ we have a foundation which cannot be moved from one location to another. We are to remain persistently and consistently on it.

In Ephesians 2:20, Paul compares the saint's life to

a building, "built on the foundation of the apostles and prophets, with Christ Jesus himself as the chief cornerstone." This implies emotional security and stability. Our feelings are not built on shifting sand. We do not have to rise and fall from joy to discouragement. A cross-oriented Christian becomes emotionally mature. He knows he is loved; that God's love will never change. He can love himself as God loves him; and new love will flow from him to others.

The Hope of the Cross and Resurrection

All of this is culminated in hope if you are "not moved from the hope held out in the gospel. This is the gospel that you heard and that has been proclaimed to every creature under heaven, and of which I, Paul, have become a servant" (Col. 1:23). Not just any gospel; not the distorted, syncretic gospel of the Gnostics; not a gospel of wishfulness. Paul speaks of a universal gospel, the good news which has spread all over the Roman Empire; the same gospel preached by Epaphras; the gospel of the cross!

Hope is an emotion. It grows out of the intellectual conviction that God is faithful, that He is all-powerful, that He intervenes for His beloved people, that He is Lord of the future, and that He is able to make all things work together for good. The Resurrection and hope ride in tandem. Peter put it clearly: "Praise be to the God and Father of our Lord Jesus Christ! In his great mercy he has given us new birth into a living hope through the resurrection of Jesus Christ from the dead" (1 Pet. 1:3).

Calvary and the empty tomb are one act of redemption that assures us not only of our forgiveness and eternal life, but that the same power is available to us. "And if the Spirit of him who raised Christ from the dead is living in you, he who raised Christ from the dead will also give life to your mortal bodies through his Spirit, who lives in you" (Rom. 8:11). We are not alone. The Lord is present with us with unexpected interventions; His timing is always perfect. He will raise us up when we are down. Death is defeated and we are alive forever. In the period between now and our graduation into glory, we are free from fear and worry. We cannot drift beyond His care.

These verses from Colossians are a prescription for emotional stability. The four basic needs with which we began are met and healed in the cross.

We need to be loved. The cross tells us that God loves us and will not let us go. It is an *authoritative* love from the Creator and ruler of the universe. It is an *unmotivated* love flowing from His pleasure in us in spite of what we have done or been. It is an *unqualified* love which cannot be dissuaded. It is a *liberating* love which sees us "perfect" in Christ, not in our imperfections. That is the healing we all need. The result is new acceptance of ourselves and an exuberant burst of love for others.

We need to be forgiven. We all fail. The emotions of regret, remorse, and self-incrimination lead to discouragement and despair. Then the cross breaks through and we are forgiven. Nothing will ever change that. The past is blotted out; the present is cleansed; the future is delivered of the fear of failure. When we do sin we need to grasp the truth that we were forgiven even before it happened! The result is liberation from the syndrome of repeated sin.

42

We need security. The cross is the foundation of assurance. We become secure only in the presence of an unchanging love. We have a confidence that emotional pressures cannot assail. We are stable and steadfast on the "Rock of Ages." "How firm a foundation, ye saints of the Lord, is laid for your faith in his excellent Word! What more can he say than to you he hath said, you who to Jesus for refuge have fled?"

We need hope. Emotional maturity is the result of a confidence for the future that is ours in the hope of the gospel.

Getting our feelings sorted out begins with these four stabilizing emotions. In that context we can get in touch with our feelings. How do you feel right now? Up, down, joyous, sad, angry, cold, warm, hostile, or peaceful? However you feel, own up to the feeling. Then refocus on the cross. Into the depths of your emotions will flow the healing love, forgiveness, security and hope that will transform how you feel about yourself, life, others and your responsibilites.

"Bless the Lord, O my soul: and all that is within me, bless his holy name. Bless the Lord, O my soul, and forget not all his benefits" (Ps. 103:1,2, *KJV*).

Especially forget not the cross!

The Purpose and Power of a Changed Life

+ + +

Colossians 1:24-29

"I am interested a little in a lot of things, but nothing has ever captivated me." This telling comment was made by a man at a Christian conference on the purpose of life and goal-setting. Along with the other participants, he had been asked to doodle on a blank sheet of paper and draw a picture of his life as he saw it. He drew a pie with many lines through it representing the multiplicity of the interests of his life.

This man's honest drawing depicts the lives of most Christians. Many interests; no captivating, motivating, and unifying purpose. Many of us would empathize. We experience the fragmenting slices of the pie of life which demand our time and energy. But why do we do what we do? What ties it all together? Often there is little unified, clear direction and reason for living. One day flows into the next; one challenge is followed by another. The years slip by. Our families, jobs, friends, churches, involvements and responsibilities pull us in a thousand directions, but there is nothing to pull us together in a consistent purpose which is expressed through all facets of our lives. There is no destiny captivating our attention and no dynamic to accomplish it.

Not so for the apostle Paul. He had both purpose and power. Behind the rivers of wisdom and creativity of his amazing life was the mainspring of a clear conviction of the reason for his being and the resources to accomplish it.

We never know a person, really, until we get beneath the surface and discover his purpose and power. Paul has given himself to us in Colossians 1:24-29. He opens his inner self in a profoundly revealing bit of autobiography. The gift of self-disclosure was given graciously to the Colossians in a language which would help them in their battle with beguiling philosophies and distorting practices. The Gnostics boasted of a secret knowledge and esoteric mysteries. Paul exposed the secret of the new life in Christ and its mysterious source of power available to all. As we read the passage, suddenly we are aware that here is the ultimate purpose against which we must measure our goals, and the exposure of available power which makes us wonder why we try to live only on our own energies.

The Liberating Secret

It is as if the Colossians had asked Paul, "Tell us your secret! Show us the mystery of your life. The philosophers here in Colosse try to make us feel insecure by implying they have some secret insight we need to add to Christ. Put it plainly and personally, Paul."

Perhaps Epaphras had asked such a question for the Colossians about Paul's sole dependence on the absolute adequacy of Christ alone. One thing is certain: Paul knew about the Colossians' conflict and difficulty. His response was an intimate and intense disclosure of his personal purpose and power.

We are astounded by the audacity of Paul's statement of his reason for living. In verse 24, he could rejoice in his sufferings in prison because of a deeper purpose which was being accomplished: "Now I rejoice in what was suffered for you." The meaning intended is that he rejoiced in the midst of suffering for the cause of Christ and His Church everywhere. The reason he could express joy in suffering was because of his identification with Christ and all of Christ's people. He felt at one with both. What he was going through was on behalf of the Church and was an expression of his unity with Christ.

The bold words leap from the page: "And I fill up in my flesh what is still lacking in regard to Christ's afflictions, for the sake of his body, which is the church" (Col. 1:24). This clarification of purpose at first alarms us and we are forced to ask, "Fill up what is still lacking in Christ's afflictions? What was lacking? Was the cross not enough? Was Paul trying to repeat rather than accept the atonement?" We have some prayerful, expository thinking to do.

The "afflictions of Christ" does not mean His once never-to-be-repeated expiatory death of atonement of the cross. Christ also suffered persecution, rejection, hostility, and misunderstanding during His ministry prior to His cross. He promised His followers nothing less in their ministry in His name: "In this world you will have trouble. But take heart! I have overcome the world" (John 16:33). "You must be on your guard. You will be handed over to the local councils and flogged in the synagogues. On account of me you will stand before governors and kings as witnesses to them" (Mark 13:9).

In the Beatitudes Christ said: "Blessed are those who are persecuted because of righteousness, for theirs is the kingdom of heaven. Blessed are you when people insult you, persecute you and falsely say all kinds of evil against you because of me" (Matt. 5:10,11).

For Paul the call to suffer was very clear. The Lord had said about him: "This man is my chosen instrument to carry my name before the Gentiles and their kings and before the people of Israel. I will show him how much he must suffer for my name" (Acts 9:15, 16). That statement, made to Ananias prior to Paul's conversion, is crucial for our understanding here because it was after Calvary and the Resurrection. Jesus already had suffered for the sins of the world and Paul would suffer for the sake of Christ's name—not as a repetition of Calvary but as an extension and expression of it.

Because of the love the Apostle received from the cross, his purpose was to also love, in spite of the suffering it would cost him. The Saviour's death for him was the driving force of his life. He wanted everyone to experience the grace of the Lord Jesus. He believed that every person and every situation needed the cross. He was compelled to proclaim Jesus as Messiah regardless of the resistance and persecution of the Jews. He would not recant even when it meant being caught in the intertwining web of Rome's misguided justice or the sophistry of Israel's leaders. The finished work of Calvary must be proclaimed at all costs. What was unfinished was the task of telling the whole world about that which had been finished.

Finishing What's Been Finished

Now let's go even deeper. The love of Christ on the cross is both the means of our salvation and the mandate of our ministry. His love is not only our message, but our motivation. Jesus said: "If anyone would come after me, he must deny himself and take up his cross and follow me" (Matt. 16:24). Our cross is the focus of our obedience, not our inconvenience, a trial of a physical malady which prompts some to say, "Well, I guess that's my cross to bear." Rather it is the relationship or circumstance in which we are called to be faithful to Christ to love with His unlimited, unchanging, giving, and forgiving love. Any person who does not know the love of the Saviour, or any situation which is unredeemed by His love, becomes the focus of our ministry. That's what's lacking and unfinished in Christ's afflictions.

The word for "complete," *antanapleroa*, means "to fill up in turn." It is Paul's turn to love the unreached as he has been loved. "What is still lacking," *ta husteremata*, means "that which is left behind, the leftovers, still to be done." Paul's agenda was to share the cross with everyone, to bring reconciliation in

48

every broken relationship, and to spread the good news to every nation.

We must pause to consider what this means to us thus far. The substitutionary atonement, Christ's death for each one of us, is complete. He took our place. He suffered for each one of us—even if you or I had been the only person alive—in Jerusalem on that awesome Friday we now call "Good." He would have had to do it if we had been the only people in the world at the time of Calvary.

We are loved and forgiven, made right with God, and freed from guilt and remorse. But the fullness of Christ's love must "fill up" the empty places in us still untouched by the cross. Any unresolved memory of failure, any unreconciled relationship with ourselves or others, and any uncommitted wish-dream for the future must be flooded with the realization and experience of the cross. The completed work of the cross must become completed within us. To do that means radical to-the-root honesty with ourselves and our Lord. We must say, "Is my whole life lived in the shadow of the cross? Is there any area or relationship of my life which is unhealed by the love of the Crucified One?"

We all experience times when we live as if Christ had not died for us. Often self-justification or defensiveness are the telltale signs that we are trying to earn what is offered as a free gift. Our words and actions often betray that we need a fresh sense of forgiveness. The lack of self-acceptance and assurance, which spills over in meager affirmation or negativism about others, shows us that the completed work of Calvary is incomplete in our personalities

49

and attitudes. But that kind of self-inventory is not easy. It requires humility and sometimes humiliation of our pride. There is a kind of suffering in that. We are crucified with Christ. We die to our arrogant self-will.

Our Ultimate Purpose

When Paul stated his purpose in his letter to the Philippians, he said it was to "know Christ and the power of his resurrection and to share in his sufferings, becoming like him in his death" and resurrection (Phil 3:10). To the end of his ministry there were dimensions of Paul that still needed to become like Christ, but he did not despair.

The more he knew of Christ, the more he realized his true self; and the more of his needy nature he recognized, the more he had to surrender over to Christ. Listen to him, "Not that I have already obtained all this, or have already been made perfect, but I press on to take hold of that for which Christ Jesus took hold of me. Brothers, I do not consider myself yet to have taken hold of it. But one thing I do: forgetting what is behind and straining to what is ahead, I press on toward the goal to win the prize for which God has called me heavenward in Christ Jesus" (Phil. 3:12-14). Paul then gives a remarkable promise: God will reveal whatever we need in order that we can accept an area which needs changing. Our task then is to ask God right now what areas or relationships need the healing of the cross.

Beyond ourselves is the world and those who do not know the depth of the forgiving love of the cross. Calvary-motivated love for them means caring, listening, accepting. Sometimes it hurts to care that much. Christ has suffered for people vicariously; we are to suffer with them unreservedly.

What does cross-centered love demand? Suddenly our own schedules, conveniences, prejudices, judgments and preferences seem ridiculous! But when we love that deeply, we become vulnerable to being hurt; our hearts are broken by the brokenness of people. We suffer the depth of the feelings of compassion and concern.

But why endure it? Paul said he suffered for the sake of the Church. I think he meant that he saw his imprisonment and trial in Rome not only as his own, but on behalf of Christianity. The future welfare of all Christians in the Roman Empire was at stake. He felt profoundly the bond of Christ's love with all Christians. His Master had loved the Church and given Himself for it. Paul could not do less.

How unlike the strange attitude among Christians today toward the Church. A rampant individualism has allowed us the luxury of thinking of the Church not as something we are but of an institution from which we gain an inspiration. Belonging to Christ has not meant belonging to a fellowship of believers. Our identification of the Church with the clergy seems to give us the liberty to go wherever we are satisfied by a particular preacher rather than being inseparably knit into a family of faith.

But Paul's suffering, to "fill up that which is behind of the afflictions of Christ in my flesh for his body's sake" (Col. 1:24, *KJV*), was also for the expansion of the Church. He wanted all people not only to know Christ and His love on the cross, but also to share the fellowship of the Church. He envisioned the Church constantly growing and expanding as the inclusive, loving demonstration of the new creation. For Paul, to be in Christ was to be in the Church.

In that light we can understand the further explanation of his purpose: "I have become its servant by the commission God gave me to present to you the word of God in its fullness" (1:25). The word "minister" means servant; "commission" here means stewardship. The Greek word is *oikonomian*, a combination of "house" and "law." Paul thought of himself as one given the responsibility of a servant, a steward of the household of God, administering the new law of grace for the family of the Church. As such, he preached and taught, counseled and guided with tender love which brought him into suffering. There is no limit to the suffering love we can sustain if we know it's for, and appreciated by, the people we love. And Paul's people were the people of God in the Church.

All this causes me to face some persistent questions that won't go away.

How am I suffering with gracious love for people who don't know the Saviour?

To what extent do I long for the Church to be expanded and built up with those who receive His cross-oriented love?

What kind of steward of the grace of God given to me for the Church have I been?

I pray that these same questions will disturb you until they are answered.

But that brings you and me to a raw edge. We have been unsettled by the challenge to "finish up the remainder of Christ's suffering for his body, the church" (1:24, *TLB*). We are convicted and concerned now. The awesome challenge cannot be ripped out of the Scriptures. We can never be the same again. But Paul does not leave us there. He has stated his purpose, now he gives us the secret of the power to accomplish it. His stewardship was to share the power available to accomplish our purpose.

Up to this point we have felt that completing what is lacking in Christ's afflictions is something we do for Christ. Our geographical and spatial misconceptions are showing. Paul goes on to correct that. Christ is not up there, or out there. We are not left alone to do our work for Him. The Apostle ushers us into the mystery, the superior knowledge hidden for ages but now available to the Colossians and us. The ministry of expressing and extending the cross is Christ's continuing ministry dwelling in us.

The Power for Our Purpose

We will miss both what this meant to the Colossians and what it can mean to us unless we realize that we are now about to take hold of the live wire of electrifying truth. The depleted, discouraged Colossians needed what Paul said about the power of the Christian life as much as we do. This neglected truth could transform our lives, enliven our churches, and energize our impotent, listless religion: "The mystery that has been kept hidden for ages and generations, but is now disclosed to the saints. To them God has chosen to make known among the Gentiles the glorious riches of this mystery, which is Christ in you, the hope of glory" (Col. 1:26,27).

The post-resurrection home of the living Lord Jesus Christ is in the mind and heart of the believer. Therefore the challenge of loving, forgiving, reconciling, and caring is not our responsibility for Christ, but His through us. We are channels through whom He moves to the estranged, sick and suffering world. We don't have to do it on our own. We are to allow Him to flow through our countenance, touch, words, expressions, compassionate acts, and empathetical identification.

The Indwelling Christ

Christ in us is the hope of glory. Glory is the manifestation of Christ. Our hope of His manifest ministry is in Him alone. That means that we become like Him in attitude, action, and reaction. Our words and nonverbal communication can be His to others. *The Living Bible* paraphrase of Colossians 1:26,27 catches this: "He has kept this secret for centuries and generations past, but now at last it has pleased him to tell it to those who love him and live for him, and the riches and glory of his plans are for you Gentiles too. And this is the secret: *that Christ in your hearts is the hope of glory.*"

This experience of the indwelling Christ has transformed both my personal life and my ministry. When I was gripped by this liberating experience it set me free from compulsive efforts to earn my status with God by being good enough. It replenished the parched places of my soul that kept my Christian life a constant dry spell. The indwelling Christ gave me all that I had previously worked to achieve, studied to understand, struggled to accomplish.

It happened when I realized that I had a purpose without power. After a few years in the ministry I was exhausted and frustrated. My preaching was biblically oriented and Christ-centered, but few lives were moved or changed. My church was well organized and highly programmed, but there was neither love nor joy among the people. Most of all, I was aware that something was wrong—missing—lacking. Years of theological education and biblical exposition had hit wide of the mark of the most crucial truth the Word contained. In my discouragement and despair, I asked Christ to tell me what was wrong.

My personal devotions, kept regularly but fruitlessly up to that time, were in John and Colossians. One day I was led to read Christ's promise that He could make His home with us (see John 14:23). Then I read these words in Colossians: "Christ in you, the hope of glory." They sounded like a trumpet blast. "That's it!" I said. I had tried to follow Christ to the best of my ability. I was a man "in Christ" as a recipient of the gift of His death and resurrection for me. I knew that I was forgiven, that death had no power over me and that I was alive forever. But now I was stunned intellectually with a truth I had missed. I was stirred emotionally by a power I had not appropriated. And most of all, I was startled by a vision of what the Christian was meant to be: the dwelling place of Christ; the glorious riverbed of the flowing streams of the living Lord!

I got on my knees and prayed, "Lord, I've missed the secret. I have been ministering for you and have not allowed you to work through me. Come live your life in me. Love through me; forgive through me;

suffer for the estranged through me; continue fresh realizations of Calvary everywhere about me.''

The result of that prayer is that I discovered guidance is not something I go to Christ to receive, but something He signals from within my mind and spirit.

Each person I met or worked with gave me a fresh opportunity to let go and allow Christ to speak and love through me. I found, and continually rediscover now, that my task is only to pray for openness to let Him through, and then to marvel at what He says and does.

Problems and difficulties are gifts for new levels of depth in experiencing the limitless adequacy of what Christ can do. What a relief it is to no longer feel that I have to find answers and solve problems to please or placate Him. He is at work in me. I know that as surely as I feel my heart beat and my lungs breathe.

But don't misread my enthusiasm. I am not suggesting that there has been no pain or suffering. The difference is that there is less of the excruciating distress caused by my previous resistance to Him, and more of the realization that the difficulties of living are but the focus of the next phase of the penetration of the power of the cross.

The Responsibility of Relinquishment

Our responsibility is not only faithfulness but also relinquishment. The liberating insight is that wherever and with whomever His grace is needed, Christ is at work. If He lives in us it follows that He will lead us into those situations and to those people who need Him most. It isn't that we discern what Christ is doing and join Him—that's a mediocre level of discipleship—but rather, it is that, when Christ takes up residence in us, He leads us into places and to people in which He can use our lives as an extension of the Incarnation.

We dare to pray, "Lord, here's my mind, think your thoughts in me. Be my wisdom, knowledge, and insight. Here is my voice. You told me not to worry about what I am to say, but that it would be given me what to say and how to say it. Free me to speak with silence or with words, whichever is needed. Give me your timing and tenderness. Now Lord, here is my body. Release creative affection in my face, my touch, my embrace. And Christ, if there is something I am to do by your indwelling presence, however menial or tough, control my will to do it."

We can pray, "Lord, I am ready now to be your manifest intervention in situations to infuse joy, affirm growth, or absorb pain and aching anguish. I plan to live this day and the rest of my life in the reality of you in me. Thank you for making it so!"

I am convinced that this was the reality in which Paul lived daily in his spectacular ministry. "We proclaim him, counseling and teaching everyone with all wisdom, so that we may present everyone perfect in Christ" (Col. 1:28). The word for perfect is *teleion* from *teleios* which means "perfect" or "fulfilling its purpose"; perfection is the accomplishment of our purpose. For Paul that purpose was his desire *for all people* to participate in the continuation of the ministry of the Saviour in and through the believer.

The concluding verse of this passage is a summary: "To this end I labor, struggling with all the energy he so powerfully works in me" (1:29). This means simply: I have stated my purpose; I accomplish it daily by allowing Christ to work in me with all the powerful energy He inspires and infuses in me. *The Living Bible* catches this thrust, "This is my work, and I can do it only because Christ's mighty energy is at work within me."

Unlike the man at the conference on goals, we can say, "I have one interest that captivates me—Christ in me the hope of glory. He is my purpose and my power!"

Penetrating Prayer

+ + +

Colossians 2:1-5

The other day I received a letter of affirmation and encouragement from a man I have never met. He had heard that I was passing through a difficult period because of a distressing illness in my family. The man is a recognized world leader of the Christian faith and therefore my respect for him made his letter all the more comforting. He had heard from a friend about the dark night of the soul I was experiencing.

The letter was very personal. It shared a similar experience the writer had faced and what he had learned from it. Then he told me he would pray each day for me. He said he had prayed for God to help him know how to pray for me. Then he told me specifically how God had guided him to intercede on my behalf.

What a boost that letter was! I felt loved and uplifted. Not only was I moved by this respected leader's concern, but because I knew of his profound prayer life, I was comforted by what God put on his heart to pray for me. The Lord was the initiator. He told the man what He was desirous of giving me so he would know what to ask for in his prayers. The letter was not only from this concerned prayer warrior, it was a message from God Himself!

The Quality of Concern

I now know how the Colossians felt when they read this next section of Paul's letter recorded in chapter 2:1-5. It was because of who Paul was, the quality of his concern for them, and what he prayed for them that brought them fresh hope and strength. This passage helps us to learn how to pray for the people the Lord places on our hearts.

Epaphras had gotten through to Paul about the Colossians' need and registered on his mind the real crisis of faith and practice with which they were grappling. In response Paul says: "I want you to know how strenuously I am exerting myself for you" (Col. 2:1). Note the meaning of "strenuously exerting." One translation uses the word "strive." The Greek is *agona* from which we derive our word "agony." Paul agonized in prayer for the church at Colosse and nearby Laodicea. It was not a flippant, flash prayer. Prolonged, penetrating intercession and attentive, receptive listening for God's answer on what to pray for distinguished the Apostle's prayer life. He allowed God to put the Colossians on his heart. He really cared. The agony was not to get God's attention, but to sort out the implications of the Lord's attentiveness.

The Vital Vocation

Prayer is the vital vocation of the Christian. We have the privilege of sharing God's work in the world. I am convinced that our Lord has ordained that His blessings and power for us are dependent upon the prayers of others. It is as if He asks, "How much do you care? How deeply are you willing to go in your intercession? How can you ask for a costly gift for another which has cost you so little time and energy in prayer?"

I find that the greatest part of prayer for others is patient, persistent communion, and waiting for the picture of what God wants us to dare to ask. It's one thing to commit a person to God in a hasty half-minute prayer. It's something else to set aside a long period of silence. I find that it's helpful to take a clean sheet of paper and write at the top the concern which brings us to prayer for another person. Then praise God in advance for His guidance and grace; thank Him that He will use you as an agent of His intervention, then be quiet! Now trust Him to guide your writing. I am always amazed at the insight and vision I receive which I could never have produced by myself.

The result of Paul's striving in prayer for the Colossians helps us understand not only what God wanted to give the Colossians, but also what He wants to give you and me and the people for whom we agonize in prayer. We will mine the treasures of this passage if we take a trilateral approach of what it meant to the Christians in the Lycus Valley, to us personally, and to the people for whom we have a God-given concern.

Prayer for Encouragement

Paul prayed first that "they may be encouraged in heart" (Col. 2:2). That's an exciting request. The word encouraged has several meanings which flow from the Greek word *paraklesios*. The *Paraclete* is the Holy Spirit. Jesus promised the gift of the Spirit, the "Comforter," who would bring to our remembrance all that Jesus said and did for us. The Comforter would stand beside us as sustainer and come within us as strengthener.

The word *paraclete* also describes Jesus' intercessory ministry on our behalf. John makes this clear: "We have an advocate with the Father, Jesus Christ the righteous" (1 John 2:1, *KJV*). "Advocate" is another translation of the word *paraclete*. Jesus is like a defense lawyer. *The Living Bible* catches the impact of this: "But if you sin, there is someone to plead for you before the Father. His name is Jesus Christ."

The word *paraclete* also carries the implication of exhortation, the urging of the next step of growth in Christ. When Paul prayed that the Colossians be comforted, he wanted all the ministry of the living Christ, the Holy Spirit, in their lives. He had claimed the same blessing for the Corinthians: "Praise be to the God and Father of our Lord Jesus Christ, the Father of compassion and the God of all comfort, who comforts us in all our troubles, so that we can comfort those in any trouble with the comfort we ourselves have received from God" (2 Cor. 1:3,4).

It is fascinating to note that Barnabas was called a son of encouragement (see Acts 4:36). Again the same Greek word is used. He brought Christ's strength, he exhorted people to grow, he mediated forgiveness and strengthened people who were weak. Acts tells about his gift of encouragement when he came to Antioch: "When he arrived and saw the evidence of the grace of God, he was glad and encouraged them all to remain true to the Lord with all their hearts" (Acts 11:23). Barnabas was a comforter, an affirmer, a gracious challenger, and a source of strength.

In a very real way Barnabas' fellow emissary and adventurer, Paul, was being a son of encouragement in his letter to the Colossians. He longed for his friends, known to him through Epaphras, to have the energizing strength, assurance, and growth of the living Christ in them. What he had experienced himself he wanted for them.

That's a sure and powerful prayer for people. If they have the indwelling Christ they will have everything else they need. And God wants to give the gift even more than we dare to ask. When the gift has been our own experience, we will long for the people in our prayers to receive it also.

Prayer for Unity

Next, Paul prays that they will be "united in love" (Col. 2:2). Unity was needed for them as individuals and in their relationships in the church. There is no finer prayer for people and the Church. Love unifies and heals. Love is the power to forgive and be reconciled. Our relationships with one another are the acid test of how much we have allowed Christ to love us. Jesus prayed that we might be one even as He and the Father were one. This prayer, prayed on the night before He was crucified (see John 17). He has continued to pray through the ages and is still praying for us and our churches.

There is no greater contradiction to the Church's message than the misunderstanding that is tolerated among its members. The human power struggle is at work in all relationships. The question of control, of who is in charge, disrupts and divides. Jesus challenged that "All men will know that you are my disciples if you love one another" (John 13:35).

It's difficult to pray that people be knit together in love if we are unraveled with discord ourselves. Praying for others prompts the Lord's questions in our quiet: "Have you the gift you're asking for others? Where do you need reconciling love in your own life? Don't ask for a blessing you are not accepting yourself!" That forces me to list out the people to whom I need to be knit in love.

I talked to a great Methodist preacher who told me about his preparation to preach on reconciliation. Suddenly nine people in his congregation were riveted on his mind. He was out of fellowship and communication with these people. He could not preach until he gave or asked for forgiveness. Some tough restitution with a couple of them was required. When he got up to preach he told the congregation what had happened to him. The exposition sparkled and shone with personal power because it was freshly real to the communicator. He wanted for his congregation what had happened to him.

The same was true for Paul. As he sat in his quarters in Rome, dictating his letter to the Colossians, he was very aware of what God's love meant to him as it was expressed through Timothy, Luke, Aristarchus, Epaphroditus, Tychicus, and all the others. He knew he could not make it without them. But he also knew he was never meant to. That's why he loved the body of Christ, the Church, so much. He desired the same love for the Colossians.

And we are left to wonder what greater gift could be given to the churches of which we are a part. Then we must ask, "What is the Lord asking me to do and say to start the liberating process of love in my congregation?" It may start in the church school class, small group or committee in which we participate. "Lord, begin with me and my relationships. What I want for my church, start with me!" Be bold to pray like that!

Prayer for the Riches of Understanding

Next, Paul wants the Colossians to have "the full riches of complete understanding, in order that they may know the mystery of God, namely, Christ, in whom are hidden all the treasures of wisdom and knowledge" (Col. 2:2,3). Most of the problems we face and about which we pray for others are related to lack of understanding of Christ—what He did, what it means to us, and what is available to us through Him.

Paul reminds the Colossians of the riches of Christ. His life, message, death, resurrection, and present power are His riches. All the love, forgiveness, power, and peace needed comes from Him. The mystery he has been talking about, which immensely superseded the mysteries of the Gnostic philosophies, was open to them. The hidden treasures have been found; the treasure chest is open. Not just some of the treasures of wisdom and knowledge are offered in Christ, but everything we could ever want or need. The key to unlock the treasures is faith in Christ Himself. Along with the Colossians we can have the rich experience of knowing Christ with certainty, understanding, and assurance. Doubt and vacillation can be replaced by an unassailable security.

I am interested in the fact that as I consider the people for whom I pray, this assurance is one of the most powerful gifts for which I need to pray. I sense that the insecurity and instability of most of the Christians I am concerned about is because of their unsure relationship with Christ. Paul's prayers for the Colossians force me to get to the taproot of that need. I am amazed by the promise that my prayer is an absolutely necessary step in the release of the gift in people. That's an awesome motivation to pray consistently and faithfully. You may find it helpful to list out the people in your scope of influence who need the gift of full assurance of understanding and the experience of the mystery of Christ's treasures. Carry this list with you. Pray often during each day. God will respond. He is the author of the prayer in our minds and hearts. He is ready to answer.

But the problems of the Colossians were not limited to those within them or between them; the Colossians were under attack from outside. As we have seen, the Gnostics were relentless in their pressures on the Christians and the Church. Paul was concerned that no one deceive them with "fine-sounding arguments" (2:4). The Greek means to "reason along side," with "persuasive speech." The danger was that the philosophers were trying, in very forceful language, to add to Christ's ideas. It was this mixture of the gospel with Gnostic philosophy that Paul feared most.

It is no different today. The people on our hearts are constantly tempted to add theories, values, economic presuppositions and cultural patterns to the gospel and baptize them with equal importance with the lordship of Christ. Often these beliefs are those we had before we came to Christ, as well as some we have added to Him which distort and dilute the gospel.

Nationalism, denominationalism, and unscriptural theological assumptions can become more important than Christ. Also, in our time of astrology, occultism, and transcendental meditation, we can be led into side ventures which seem to be an expression of our basic faith but can eventually become diminutive gods. Christ is thoroughly adequate for all our needs. But when we drift from the essential relationship with Him we become prey to eccentric distortions: We are away from our center in Christ. Luther was right: "Man only needs Christ!"

Prayers of Affirmation

Finally, Paul's prayers for the Colossians lead into renewed affirmation. We all need insight into what we are to do and encouragement for what we have been doing. Everyone needs love expressed in gracious accolades for our efforts to attempt the very things the Lord desires for us to realize. Paul wanted the Colossians to know he was aware of how well they were doing in the battle. That would give them the courage and strength to "keep on keeping on."

He is overjoyed by the reports of "how orderly you are and how firm your faith in Christ is" (2:5). The Apostle uses military language. "Orderly" is *taxis*, a military term for an orderly lineup of soldiers. The word firm is *stereoo*, meaning "to make the line solid," like a phalanx. In that time soldiers, with shields held in place and spears positioned, moved in against an enemy's columns with an inverted V-like array. Then the break through the lines enabled them to turn and attack from within the enemy's forces. Paul affirmed that the Colossians were not only standing fast; their steadfastness was an attack on the opposing enemies.

The most creative way to empower a person is to undergird his efforts with encouragement for how well he is doing. That fires a renewed dedication to battle on. We can only imagine how uplifted the Colossians were by Paul's recognition of their efforts.

This passage has made us do a lot of thinking about how to pray for the people of our lives. We have a good basis for an incisive inventory of our prayers. Do the people for whom we pray know it? And knowing that we do pray, are they aware of the depths of our intercessions? It could make all the difference for them. The prayers of people have changed my life and made it an adventure. How about you?

The Fullness to Fill the Emptiness

+ + +

Colossians 2:6-12

I gave my life to Christ as my Lord when I was a freshman in college. I never will forget the joy I experienced when I got down on my knees in my dormitory room and thanked Him for His love and forgiveness on the cross. In response to His acceptance of me just as I was, I surrendered my will and the control of my future. It was the beginning of a relationship which has continued to grow every day of the years since.

Christ is Christianity to me. He is everything to me—He means everything and He provides everything I need to know to live fully. He has given me purpose and power; He has guided in success and failure; He has sensitized all of my life with adventure and excitement; and He has defeated fear of life's eventualities and anxiety about death's power. He has never failed me when I trusted Him with my family or my work. His interventions have always been on time—never ahead of time, never late. Often in times of frustration, He has untangled the snarls of my human inadequacy. His love has enabled me to fall deeply in love with people. My passion for Him has impassioned me to spend my life telling others about Him. Life in Christ has not always been easy, but it has never been dull!

And yet I realize that I barely have begun to know Christ! I have spent 27 years in colleges, seminaries, universities and daily study, and I still feel like a beginner. Intellectually, I am still a freshman when it comes to fathoming the fullness of who He is, what He came to do, what He said, how He reconciled the world, and what He continues to do today through the Holy Spirit.

Emotionally, I long to experience the complete healing of my memories and a further liberation of my feelings in order to more completely receive and express love. On the volitional level, I long to grow in obedience to discover and follow His guidance. The amazing thing about life in Christ is that we're never finished growing. If I am given the gift of a long life, I probably will feel like a beginner in old age. It takes a lifetime, and then all of eternity, to understand, respond, experience, and appropriate the riches of Jesus Christ; and yet I know all I need to know right now. He is my Saviour and Lord. But I know very little in comparison to what He wants me to discover. All of life is the laboratory of that learning. And I am thankful.

Assurance and Aspiration

Assurance and aspiration were carefully balanced by the Apostle. He desired the Colossians to be sure

70

of their salvation and still be eager to grow. They had arrived, and yet the journey of faith had only begun. He wanted to assure them of their settled status as the Lord's people, but he also wanted to startle them with how little they knew of the One who loved them so much.

"So then, just as you received Christ Jesus as Lord, continue to live in him, rooted and built up in him, strengthened in the faith as you were taught, and overflowing with thankfulness" (Col. 2:6,7). It's a challenge to keep up with Paul's metaphors. Here he uses two to encourage the Colossians to continue to grow up in Christ. He tells them to put their roots down into Christ—a powerful image. Christ is the totally adequate source of their new life. The deeper their roots grow in the rich, resourceful soil of Christ Himself, the stronger their Christian life will be.

Next, he refers to Christ as the foundation of the building of their Christian experience. He alone is the sure foundation for Christian living in a place like Colosse—or Los Angeles—or your town. Paul gives us the only hope of survival: Christ and fellowship with Him. He is all we need. With Him we have all things; without Him all the things we have amount to nothing.

Keep Alert

The Colossians were to be constantly alert, on the lookout with a watchful eye, for ever-present temptation to make unnecessary additions or substitutions to the gospel: "See to it that no one takes you captive through hollow and deceptive philosophy, which depends on human tradition and the basic principles of this world rather than on Christ" (Col. 2:8). Good advice! There was constant danger if the new Christians failed to keep centered in Christ. The word captive is *sulagogeo*, "to carry off" as a captive or slave. The Gnostic philosophers were ready to claim the Christians as their spoil.

Paul is not down on philosophy, great learning, or intellectual growth. Philosophy, as the love of wisdom, has meant enrichment and stimulating thought to many of us. The danger comes when basic assumptions are established which are in contradiction to the gospel. Man cannot think himself through to reality. Christ is our reality. Right thoughts do not make us righteous. Only the cross can do that. The "good" is not an achievement but the gift of the goodness of God. Philosophic discipline forces us to think clearly, but it is ultimately insufficient in enabling the abundant life or assuring us of eternal life. Christ alone can fill the emptiness.

In Colosse, the beguiling philosophy was a maze of distorted thinking about both God and man and how they could be brought into relationship. The new Christians needed to be constantly alert to the subtle mixture of Christian thought with false philosophy. So do Christians today.

False Philosophies Today

Consider these ideas, false philosophies, which are pervading our culture: God helps those who help themselves; He will love us more if we are good; He will judge us according to our accomplishments; Anything that feels good must be good; Self-expression is the only way to self-realization; Enjoyment is enrichment; Christ is the best of all good men—an example of living for us, nothing more; What we are is what we acquire; Our worth is determined by our productivity . . . .

And so it goes. Everything—from the playboy philosophy to materialism, astrology to scientism, sensualism to sorcery—is seeking to possess the American mind to manipulate our behavior and motivate our spending. And often Christians are among those who respond because their emptiness has not been filled by the fullness of Christ. His fullness fills our emptiness.

The Fullness of God

Paul meets the problem of the Christian's emptiness in one of the most comprehensive and stirring statements in Scripture about Christ: "For in Christ all the fullness of the Deity lives in bodily form, and you have this fullness in Christ, who is the head over every power and authority" (Col. 2:9,10).

Nothing has been left out, unrevealed, or unexposed. The word "fullness" is the same as we considered in chapter 1:19: *pleroma*, plenitude, the entire fullness of the Godhead. All we can or need to know about God, He has made known in Christ. No need for speculation or search for other answers. Christ is the full and final revelation of God and man as He was intended to be. God dwelt in the flesh in Christ, made His home in Him and now continues to dwell in Him as His persistent approach to us. What else do we need? Why search for our meaning for life elsewhere? Why create additional intermediaries or intercessors? That's what Paul wanted the Colossians to settle once and for all. And so must we.

What Fills Our Emptiness?

To feel the full implication of this message we need
to be honest about the things we add to Christ for our
security. He is not the fullness of God for us if we
continue to need something or someone else to fill
the emptiness. Paul assures us that from the fullness
of God in Christ we have fullness. It's one thing to
accept the fullness of God in the Incarnation and
quite another to be filled with the fullness of Christ.
We can be doctrinally pure but spiritually empty.

The issue is allowing what God did in Christ to
have pervading influence on all of life and every relationship. That means spelling out His lordship in very
practical terms for every facet of life. And that's how
we "continue to live in him." Paul's prayer for the
Ephesians offers the same promise he gave to the
Colossians: "That Christ may dwell in your hearts
through faith. And I pray that you, being rooted and
established in love, may have power, together with all
the saints, to grasp how wide and long and high and
deep is the love of Christ, and to know this love that
surpasses knowledge—that you may be filled to the
measure of the fullness of God" (Eph. 3:17-19).

How Christ Fills Our Emptiness

How can this happen? How can the fullness of
Christ fill our emptiness? Paul gives us the secret in
Colossians 2:11,12. It will be repeated various times
in the remainder of the letter in several different con-
texts. The repetition will be helpful in making the
awesome truth crystal clear. We enter into the full-

ness of Christ and the fullness of His Spirit enters into us through participation in His death and resurrection. Our baptism is a death and resurrection experience. "In baptism you were buried with him and raised with him [Christ] through your faith in the power of God" (2:12).

Baptism in the early Church was an outward sign of surrender to Christ and being raised up to a new life. This recapitulation of Christ's death and rising may occur at the time of our baptism or, as is often the case, when we die in our plans and purposes and receive the power of the Resurrection for a new level of life in union with Him. In my own case, my baptism as an infant was not appropriated by me until that night in my college room. The same often is true for people who have had a believer's baptism as teenagers or adults. That should be the time of their death and resurrection as they are lowered into the water and raised up to newness of life. In reality, however, the experience of the death of self often occurs later when life's problems or potentials drive a person to trust Christ completely. It is not so important *when* it happens, but *that* it happens.

The crucial need in all of us is the baptism of the Holy Spirit, the living Christ. When we open our lives—mind, heart and will—giving Christ the control of our lives, He enters in to live His life in and through us. That's when the joy and power to live the Christian life are given to us. We begin to experience the fullness of Christ as He takes charge and runs our lives. Amazing! Awesome! The reason we were born!

Verse 12 has helped us to understand verse 11: "In him you were also circumcised, in the putting off of your sinful nature, not with a circumcision done by the hands of men but with the circumcision done by Christ." Circumcision was the sign of the old covenant of Moses and a Hebrew male's identification with the Law. Paul is now talking about an inner circumcision of the heart done by Christ. We belong to Him and, in response, have put off our "sinful nature." The words are decisive; they mean "to strip off, completely put away." The important thing is that our old self-centered nature is replaced by a new Christ-centered nature. A completely new and different disposition, attitude and pattern of thought. Christ Himself becomes our new nature. The same liberating, empowering promise we considered in 1: 27: "Christ in you, the hope of glory." Paul won't let us forget that. His mind will return to the triumphant truth again in subsequent sections of the epistle.

A Personal Question

For now, at this stage of our study, I want to have us personalize this truth for ourselves. How did you react to what Paul offered the Colossians in these very vital verses we have considered? Is it real to you? Has Christ filled your emptiness? If not, what are you attempting to fill this void with that leaves little room for Him? We dare not end this day without answering both questions.

Nailing It Down
+ + +
Colossians 2:13-15

Would you consider yourself a free person? On what basis would you make your evaluation? What would you say makes a free person? Whom do you know who qualifies as a liberated personality?

These questions force us to define what we mean by freedom. I have found that the truly free people I know have four ingredients of liberty. They have dealt with the past and are free from incriminating memories of failure; they have had an experience of forgiveness which has extricated them from self-condemnation; they have been unfettered from the bonds of compulsive patterns; and they are emancipated from dependence on the opinions and criticism of people. From these basic elements flows the freedom to accept and love ourselves, give affirmation and esteem to others, and live with confidence about the future.

Freedom of Fellowship

This quality of freedom can be known only in fellowship with Christ. Yet I am painfully aware that there are many Christians who believe in Christ, but who are not free. The remarkable thing is that many church people can hear the gospel, sing about the cross, and pray for guidance and still be bound and uptight. The great need is to experience the dynamic of the cross for our personal liberation from the failures of the past and the disturbing memories of what might have been.

That's exactly what Paul wanted for the Colossians. They had accepted Christ, but were still distressed by mistakes and misdeeds of the past. Added to that, they were being unsettled by the criticisms of others who demanded that they live up to their standards. Something had to be written to them to establish them on a firm foundation. And it would have to be communicated in vivid, pictorial language which would break the chains of the past.

A Portrait of Freedom

Paul was a master communicator—he could paint pictures with words which were packed with emotion and reorienting truth. In Colossians 2:13-23 we have Paul's portrait of the cross as the basis of Christian freedom. A careful study of the powerful images in these verses unlocks the prisons of the past and helps us to breathe the fresh air of our deliverance. When we are free of the past and when we stop demeaning ourselves, then we can live free from the debilitating demands of others.

Some background on this particular passage will help. The Colossian Christians were the victims of not only the Gnostic philosophies but of the Jews who maintained that an impeccable fulfillment of the Law—the Ten Commandments plus the annotated rules and regulations—was required to earn a right relationship with God. What God had given to guide the behavior of His people had been twisted to be the basis of self-justification. The problem was about what to do with the infractions of the Law and the man-made regulations. It was an old problem. Jesus had dealt with it in the Sermon on the Mount; Paul was confronted with it everywhere he went in the expansion of the Church. It's our frustration also.

What to Do with "the Oughts"

The basic ethical and moral behavior demanded by the commandments is a part of the "ought" which dominates our life. But even a quick review of the requirements of the commandments forces us to realize that we have failed miserably. Guilt and a condemning conscience result. We then try to deal with that by either saying, "Well, nobody's perfect, why try?" or "I'm going to be good enough to deserve God's approval!" The outcome is either license or perfectionism. Neither works. Both result in an uneasy state of grace. In either case we are faced with the realization of our failures. What can we do about them? That's what the Colossian Christians wanted to know. And so do we.

Paul's answer is one of the most potent passages in

the New Testament. His spectacular rhetoric opens windows through which we can look at the truth and appropriate it.

Identification with Christ

The first picture Paul paints is to help us identify with Christ. His affirmation of true Christian freedom is rooted in an incisive identification with Christ in His death and resurrection. This is a familiar, oft-repeated, favorite theme of the Apostle. Actual union with Christ in His death is the only way to deal with the past: "When you were dead in your sins and in the circumcision of your sinful nature" (Col. 2:13). By that, Paul means not only "trespasses," *paraptoma*, but "inner motivation of our carnal, human nature," *akrobustia tes sarkas*. Separation from God through our rebellious acts and inner heart makes us dead to what life was intended to be. We become the walking dead.

The Triumphant Transaction

Recognition of what life was like prior to meeting Christ prepares us to accept the need for the cross. But it also makes way for the triumphant transaction of the Resurrection: "God made you alive with Christ" (2:13). Resurrection is the realized "now" experience of the Christian. The Greek words are filled with meaning. We are quickened, made alive together in Christ. The cross is the definite demarcation between the old life and the beginning of the new. When Christ died, we died; when He was raised up, we were resurrected. The cross and the empty tomb stand between us and the haunting memory of the past. All our failures are focused through the victory of Calvary and Easter morning.

In Romans 6, the emancipation is undeniably explained and given full force: "We were therefore buried with him through baptism into death in order that, just as Christ was raised from the dead through the glory of the Father, we too may live a new life. If we have been united with him in his death, we will certainly also be united with him in his resurrection. For we know that our old self was crucified with him so that the body of sin might be rendered powerless, that we should no longer be slaves to sin—because anyone who has died, has been freed from sin . . . . In the same way, count yourselves dead to sin but alive to God in Christ Jesus" (Rom. 6:4-7,11).

In Time for All Time

To grasp the full meaning of "all time" we need a fresh understanding of time. God exists beyond time and is the same yesterday, today and tomorrow. He is not limited to our calculation of hours, days and years. In Christ He has revealed His forgiving love for all time. In any moment, the cross and the empty tomb are God's attitude toward us. Though these events occurred 2000 years ago, they are the propitious offer of changeless grace in this moment of time. When Christ died He atoned for all sin, before and after, in all time. In that context we can own what we have been and disown it because of what God has done. There can be no lasting freedom without that.

Clearing the Charge List

Now we are ready to press on to Paul's next illuminating illustration. He pictures the Colossians' sins as a charge list. In ancient times charges were listed out against a person and if he signed it, that was an admission in his own hand of his debt. The Greek word for a charge list was *cheirographon*, meaning an "autograph, a note of hand, a bond."

In Paul's time, people wrote on papyrus, made of the pith of bulrushes, or on vellum, made of the skin of animals. The ink used then had no acid in it and therefore did not penetrate indelibly into the fiber of the paper. A sponge could wipe it away as if it had never existed on the surface.

In that context, we can picture what a radical redemption Paul wanted to portray: "He [God] forgave us all our sins, having canceled the written code, with its regulations, that was against us and that stood opposed to us" (Col. 2:13,14). The word canceled is *exaleipho*, "to wipe off, wipe away, obliterate, erase." The law had established the code of conduct and the Colossian Christians, like all of us, had failed to live up to all its standards. The charge list is the composite tabulation of all that we have said and done, or should have said and done. Anything come to mind? Can you make up a list? I can! What can we do about it? We could not dare to see ourselves as we are, or have been, without also knowing that God has taken the grace sponge of the cross and blotted out all the charges, wiping the page clean of all the incriminating, acknowledged failures.

The Slate Is Clean

You and I are completely exonerated! Our slate is clean before God. Allow the full impact of that to pervade and penetrate your mind and heart. As far as God is concerned He relates to us as if we had never sinned! Because of Christ and the cross, He has a poor memory; in fact, He has no memory at all when it comes to our sins.

The problem is that most of us have a better memory than God has! We are far less gracious to ourselves than He is. That's blasphemy. We harbor the mistakes and misdeeds long after we have heard and seemingly accepted the good news of the gospel. We continue to assume the responsibility for our self-justification even though God assumed it once and for all on Calvary. It is as if we say to God, "You are far too generous; you may forgive us but we will repeat a Calvary of our own, thank you! We'd rather do it ourselves."

Sounds absurd doesn't it? Yet we do it all the time. Guilt drives us to all sorts of patterns, actions, and activities to prove our self-worth, in spite of what we are. What do you do to assure yourself that you are of value when you know your behavior has devalued what you were meant to be? We often live as if Calvary had not happened!

The Absolute Adequacy of the Cross

The Colossians must also have lived as if Calvary had not happened. That's the reason Paul enlarges his illustrative picture of the absolute adequacy of the cross with an image that is even more unforgettable. God not only sponged the charge list clean, "He took it away, nailing it to the cross" (2:14). The original language is drastic. It means that God wrenched the charge list out of the people's clenched fists. He took

83

it completely away from us. It's not ours anymore; it belongs to Him now. What He did with it is what forces us to accept our forgiveness.

Nailed to the Cross

He nailed it to the cross! Often a charge list against a person, signed with his own name, was nailed publicly. When the debts were paid or the charges exonerated, the nail cutting through the list was the seal and sign of the cancellation of the debt or charge. Paul builds on this picture in a very dramatic way. When the nails were driven through Christ's hands and feet, all our sins were crucified with Him. The Lord was our charge list nailed to the cross! Our sins and failures were cut clean through by the nails which caused the Saviour such anguish.

He took the sins of the whole world, then and now—yours and mine. When He cried, "It is finished!" He declared not only the finished work of redemption but the finish of our hostility to ourselves for the past. More than that, when Christ was crucified, the law and all its demands were nailed to the cross. Now we are free to fulfill the law motivated by the love of the cross, not to establish our righteousness but because we are right before God through the cross. We desire to do God's commandments not in order to have God love us, but because He already does so with grace that will never change.

We will catch the full dynamic of this if we are able to take all of the memories of failures and nail them to the cross. It is an act of confession and assurance of forgiveness. God wants to heal our memories so that we can live the abundant life without reservation. Nailing our sins to the cross should become a daily discipline. Sins should be dealt with decisively. If we pile up the sins of our yesterdays and add the pressures of today we will break down. Nailing them to the cross each day is a radical confrontation with our Lord that results in a remedial confidence.

We need to do the same with the things people do which hurt us. Before we retaliate in an effort to balance the scales, we should take the wrong done to us and nail it to the cross. Nail it down! Then we can forgive what the Lord has forgiven. We will have no power to do that without the continuing experience of the Lord's forgiveness of us. It is sheer arrogance to refuse to forgive in another person what the Lord has forgiven. There is no freedom without forgiveness of ourselves and others.

Set Free

The cross was not only a once never-to-be-repeated atonement for our sins, it was also a victory over the elemental spirits, angels and demons. We are set free from both self-incrimination and "spirit" condemnation. The Gnostic belief in a graduation of angels between God and man, which we talked about earlier, is confronted again in verse 15. Not all of these angels were benign. The belief was that some of them actually were agents of evil. Paul wants the Colossians to know that all of these "powers and authorities," the malignant and hostile forces, had been disarmed and defeated. Christ had done battle with evil and stripped it of all power over the Christian. Possession by these malicious foes was no longer possible for a person in Christ.

The Conquering Christ

The picture in Paul's mind is of a conquering general with his defeated enemies in his train. It was the practice in those days for a victorious general to march his captives through the streets to expose their impotence as his prisoners.

In our own time of reemphasis on Satan and demon possession we need to think clearly about what Christ's victory means. The Christian is sealed in Jesus' name against any invasion of Satan or demons. We do not need to live our lives in constant fear of Satan's power. By constantly focusing our attention on Christ and opening our lives to His indwelling power, we share His victory.

Satan's weapons are discouragement and dissemblement. Paul wants us to know that having dealt with self-incrimination, we are also free of Satan's indictments. We are free from forces within and without.

Complete Freedom

We have come full circle back to where we began in this chapter. Now we know what complete freedom is and can discern the extent to which we have become free persons. Sin has been nailed to the cross; the enemies of life defeated. Now we are free to live the new life with abandonment and joy!

Christianity Is More Than Do's and Don'ts

+ + +
Colossians 2:16-23

One of the most difficult challenges for Christians in every age is to remain in vital union with Christ in the midst of cultural religion. Every nation and community has its values, beliefs and practices which contradict the lordship of Christ and our absolute loyalty to Him. Christians have always been distinguished for daring to follow Christ and not the distorted, distracting ideas in a culture of what life is to be. The pressure to conform is often unbearable and painful.

The Colossians had a particularly difficult time. They were being threatened by the Gnostics. The equivocative philosophers and their confused followers were using a very powerful, unsettling tool. They were questioning the Christian's morality and religious sincerity. They held to cherished rules and regulations, coupled with customs and beliefs, which the Christians no longer found necessary in their new life in Christ. ·

The Gnostics constantly tried to put the barbed hook of guilt into the Colossian Christians' conscience about those things they no longer practiced because they were unnecessary for a liberated person filled with the Saviour. Many of us can empathize.

Religion Is Not Enough

It's not easy to be free from the "oughts" of previous religious compulsions and conditioning. Long after we are set free in Christ, the old memory tapes are replayed with guilt-producing regularity.

I was raised in a church atmosphere in which, to my adolescent mind and sensitive spirit, following Christ and remembering the things I should not do were blended into one admonition. Often the don'ts were all I heard. To be a Christian meant not being able to do many of the fun things most kids enjoyed. Also, there were obligations to being a Christian which were fragmented from union with Christ. I ended up with a list of demands with no dynamic to live them.

I became very hostile to man-made religion. Like the scribes of old, my religious instruction had a regulation for every situation spelled with two letters: No! Christ became a negation of the verve of life, the desire to grow intellectually and the delight of being alive. The result of the judgmentalism of the advocates of the "rules-religion" drove me from the Christ they felt they wanted me to know.

The same emotional residue, though different in content, waterlogged the spirits of the Colossian Christians. The difficulty was that they were under judgment from the religion they had left. The greatest pressure came from those who had been liberated Christians but had gone back into the bondage of Gnostic philosophy and religion. Their subtle judgment was that Christ was not enough. The both/and of Christianity and Gnosticism was the burden under which these syncretizers lived. They were more than ready to share their own uneasy guilt with the Christians to whom Paul was writing.

Freedom from Human Judgmentalism

Paul was very direct. He knew from Epaphras what was happening. "Therefore do not let anyone judge you by what you eat or drink, or with regard to a religious festival, a new moon celebration, or a sabbath day" (Col. 2:16)—cultural religion in conflict with Christ.

Old conditioning made the new Christians vulnerable. Were the Gnostics right? Or did Christ really make these things unnecessary? The assurance they had was in direct warfare with asceticism. The Gnostic disdain for matter as evil had led to a labyrinth of laws about what could and could not be eaten and drunk. In essence, they had adopted all the food laws of the Jews. The Essenes were the vigilantes of that legalism. The issue was between self-justifying asceticism and faith in Christ.

Some of the food laws were creative in themselves. Many of them would enable better health but the regulations were given equal status with the Law which, in the deeper dimensions, was being neglected in fanatic observation of the secondary rules. A further confusion in Colosse was that the obligations had been wrenched out of the Mosaic tradition. Many of the rules were attributed to angels and spirit emanations. What a confusing mess of blended religion! For the Essenes, abstinence from meat and drink was equally and finally more important than love for one's neighbor.

Holy days were set aside with special sacrifices and religious rituals. On these holy days work was suspended and no activity other than that prescribed was permitted. Few knew why they were celebrating the holy day, often not even the leaders. Sounds like culturalized religion at its worst. A sure sign that the weary bird of religious compulsion has come home to roost after a purposeless flight is that people celebrate a holiday with no experience of the reason it was instituted.

There was also fanaticism about the season of the new moon. This had absolutely no significance to the followers of the morning star, Jesus Christ Himself. To give in to the cultural pressure of anticipation of the special astrological powers of the new moon was to miss the One who brings the dawn of a new life. Astrological superstition is still around however. There are countless Christians who check their horoscopes more regularly than they pray or read the Bible.

Paul dismisses the sabbath observance as absurd in the light of the Messiah who made all days a sabbath for His people. Sabbatarianism is to miss Jesus' teaching that the sabbath was made for man, not man for the sabbath. Surely, we are to rest one day a week in reverence and recreation, but never as an end in itself. Think of the sabbath "Blue Laws" which, not long ago in our country, often became more important than Christ to some Christians.

What Paul was most concerned about is that the Christians would go back into old legalism instead of looking forward to Christ. The Mosaic Law was a foreshadow of the coming of Christ (Col. 2:17). What a tragedy to live in the shadow and miss the Messiah!

As we saw earlier, the worship of an elaborate gradation of angels not only denied the unique supremacy of Christ, but gave false pride of esoteric insight to those who believed in the multiplicity of intervening spirits. False humility is always the result of false pride. And it gives illegitimate birth to judgmentalism. It must maintain its necessary elevation by looking down on others. Paul said that those who claimed a special vision of the truth will have puffed-up, unspiritual minds: "Do not let anyone who delights in false humility and worship of angels disqualify you" (2:18). The word for disqualify is *katabrabeuo*. It means to "act as an umpire or a judge" against someone.

Vital Union with Christ

The Apostle's exposure of the false teachers is also a warning to the Christians. The defectors from the faith had "lost connection with the Head, for whom the whole body, supported and held together by its ligaments and sinews, grows as God causes it to grow" (2:19). Eccentric behavior and distorted beliefs had resulted in disconnection from Christ the Head of the Body, the Church. The same danger faced all the Colossian Christians.

Dependent and inseparable union with Christ is the only way any of us can know what's right and wrong, important or irrelevant. When we are united with Christ and through Him with one another in the Body, we can sort out creatively the implications of His lordship for our behavior, ethics and practices. God wants the Church to grow in maturity and power, not in slavish observance of regulations.

Freedom from Guilt

Paul's urgency is felt in verses 20-23. He gave the Colossians the basis of their power to withstand the guilt-engendering influence of the Gnostics and the Essenes, as well as the defected church members: "If you died with Christ to the basic principles of this world, why, as though you still belonged to it, do you submit to its rules: 'Do not handle! Do not taste! Do not touch!'?" (2:20,21). The death and resurrection cycle of the Christian life liberates us from past values and customs. We have died with Christ, and with that death all our old attitudes, compulsions and obligations died with Him. We have been raised to a new life in Christ and by His power.

A radical healing takes place when we surrender our old selves to Christ and die to what's past. The tissues of the brain are reordered around the mind of Christ. The messages we send from our minds to our emotions and will are guided by Christ. The new creation is a miracle of the indwelling Christ.

But it's possible, as we all know, to bring vestiges

of that old life into the new. There are areas of our memory bank that need to be excavated and liberated by Christ. The new life is motivated by Christ, not by "human commands and teachings" (2:22).

The Impotence of Religious Rules

Paul concludes this section by parading the impotent and defeated regulations before the Colossians. The one thing rules cannot do is engender the desire to know what is right and do it. "Such regulations indeed have an *appearance* of wisdom, with their self-imposed worship, their false humility and their harsh treatment of the body, but they lack any value in restraining sensual indulgence" (2:23, italics added). The reference to sensual indulgence is a strong illustration of the inadequacy of rules and self-effort. The city was filled with sexual license. In a way, Paul is saying, "Look, one of the problems we all face is the temptation of distorted sexual satisfaction. What have the Gnostic ideas and rigidity done about that? Nothing!"

What About Our Religious Traditions?

We are left to do some serious thinking about the religious traditions and cultural patterns that we have elevated to equality with Christ. Some of them are a natural outgrowth of obedience to Christ, but His power and presence alone can enable us to do the right thing for the right reason.

The Victorious Life

+ + +
Colossians 3:1-11

The victory of Christ's resurrection enables a victorious life. The hope of the resurrection is inseparably related to the promise of regeneration. For resurrection living there is resurrection power.

Jesus said, "Because I live you also will live" (John 14:19). Now, not just at the time of physical death. Eternal life is both quality and quantity. The settled, unshakable conviction of the apostle Paul was that the open tomb opened a life of immense possibilities. He wanted the Colossians not only to believe the power of Christ's resurrection but to claim the potential of their own. He gave them the secret of the victorious life in Colossians 3:1-4. Victorious resurrection living could be realized through a conscious, habitual pattern of thought and attitude of heart.

"Since, then, you have been raised with Christ, set your hearts on things above, where Christ is seated at the right hand of God. Set your minds on things above, not on earthly things. For you died, and your life is now hidden with Christ in God. When Christ, who is your life, appears, then you also will appear with him in glory" (3:1-4).

Resurrection Living

"You have been raised with Christ." We need to think about what that means. Unification with Christ in His death and resurrection is the key to unlock the power of the victorious life. When we can surrender our lives to Christ we are incorporated into His dying and rising. Commitment to Christ is to die to ourselves and our control of our lives. We are no longer in charge of our destiny. The self becomes the container and transmitter of the living Christ. When He comes to live in us, we experience a resurrection to a new level of living under His guidance and by His power. Pascal said, "It is one of the greatest principles of Christianity that that which happened in Jesus Christ may happen in the soul of the Christian. We have a linking not only with Calvary, but with his resurrection."

The victorious life flows from this exciting realization. Dedication to Christ begins a whole new life. Heaven, a vital union with Christ, begins now. We have a new set of desires, a new purpose, and a new perspective. That's what Paul means when he says: "You have been raised with Christ, set your hearts on things above." Heaven in our hearts is the vitality of the victorious life.

We Become What We Think

Paul knew that we become what we think about; we are inadvertently molded by the passions of our hearts. Our goals shape our priorities. Obviously, the Colossians had accepted Christ and His salvation, but their minds and hearts were still engrossed in "earthly things."

We can empathize. Long after we have begun the new life, our thoughts, energy, and time can be focused on our agenda of personal success and prosperity. This duality of direction is what debilitates so many of us. St. Augustine said, "Christ is not valued at all, unless he is valued above all." That statement bruises our both/and mentality. When many of us came to Christ we brought along our personal set of purposes, plans, and priorities. To some He became little more than an addendum to a satisfied, settled life. After commitment to Him we continued life much as it had been before: the same convictions about life, the same desires, the same attitudes. No wonder we blend so comfortably into the secular scene. Our spiritual focus is on the things above; our verve and vitality is invested on things below. Paul called for a radical transformation of attention and a reordering of values.

How to Seek the Things Above

To seek the things that are above in our obligations and responsibilities in the things on earth is the challenge of Christian living. That means recognizing that all the things on earth belong to our Lord. As participants in the Kingdom of God, we are to seek His rule and authority in our daily living. The more we focus our minds on Him, the more we will be able to use earthly things to His glory. What we can taste, touch and tabulate can never be our satisfaction. Position, popularity, and the people of our lives are not our security. But when they are, we become vulnerable candidates for discouragement and disappointment. Most of the things which upset us are the denial of desires which don't ultimately count.

The Christian can be victorious in life's difficulties because he can see them as transitory and absolutely incapable of separating him from his heavenly purpose. That's why Paul could say, "I consider that our present sufferings are not worth comparing with the glory that will be revealed in us ... Who shall separate us from the love of Christ? Shall trouble or hardship or persecution or famine or nakedness or danger or sword? ... No, in all these things we are more than conquerors through him who loved us. For I am convinced that neither death nor life, neither angels nor demons, neither the present nor the future, nor any powers, neither height nor depth, nor anything else in all creation, will be able to separate us from the love of God that is in Christ Jesus our Lord!" (Rom. 8:18,35,37-39).

A woman once came to Ralph Waldo Emerson and said that the world was coming to an end. To which Emerson replied, "That's all right, I can get along without it." And so can we! The realization frees us to live with joy and delight. We can creatively love only what we do not need.

One of America's most famous and popular movie actors expressed to me the essence of the victorious life. "I never believed that either my talents or opportunities were anything but a gift. God gave them to me and I have used them for His glory. Disappointments, and what some people call frustrations, were only transitions so that I could see a new direction. If I hold fast to my conviction that Christ is in charge and knows what He's doing with me, how can I doubt His loving reordering of my life? When I surrendered having to succeed, I could handle success." Exactly! This man has broken through to freedom.

Diminutive Deaths

As a pastor I listen to people in life's excruciating pressures and problems and I have come to the conviction that most of the things which tear us apart are caused by divided loyalties between Christ and our own agenda. Each defeat, setback, loss, or personal tragedy is a little death. Because we have not settled our own dying and claimed that we are alive forever in Christ, each diminutive death is shocking. Our reaction to life's eventualities exposes the sources of security.

A fine churchwoman said, "When my husband died, it was as if I died with him. I can't imagine life without him!"

A leader in a church said, "I've lost my job and that means years of hard work down the drain. I feel kind of dead inside." How could this man have missed the gospel all through the years of church work?

A middle-aged single woman said, "As the years have gone by, I have lived with the hope I would be married. Now I've given up hope. What's there left to live for?"

A man suffering a battle with cancer said. "This

illness has put everything into perspective. Though I believe in Christ, I realize that I have put all my thinking and energy into my career and the standard of living it afforded. In this crisis I have met the Saviour about whom I have heard so much in church for so long. How sad that I've missed the years with Him!"

This man and thousands of others like him in American Christianity have sung "Turn your eyes upon Jesus," and yet the things of earth have not grown strangely dim for most of us. That's why we miss the victory!

The Crucial Question

The only way to allow Paul's admonition to the Colossians to get at us where we really live is to question what could happen to us that would shake our faith in our Lord. What "things of earth" would you find it difficult to do without? A loved one, a position, a financial security, a sameness with no dramatic change of circumstances? What blocks your vision of the things above?

Face it squarely. What if you were to die before this day is ended. Are you sure of where you would spend eternity? Would your death be little more than a transition in eternal living? Are you sure? If you are, you can face anything!

If death has been disarmed for us, there's reason to celebrate Christ's victory and our own. Our hope is sure. We are alive forever.

Hidden with Christ

"For you died, and your life is now hidden with

Christ in God" (Col. 3:3). We suspect that "hidden with Christ" is a play on the familiar Greek phrase "hidden in the earth," used for a person who is dead and buried. The Christian who has died spiritually is hidden in Christ. But the implication probably means something further. The Gnostics took great pride in their possession of hidden mysteries of God. They claimed hidden books of wisdom, esoteric, understood by only the initiated few. What Paul may have meant was that the hidden secret of life in Christ belonged to the Christians. Through their death with Christ, they had found the secret of the resurrected life of power and victory.

Christ Is Our Life

The last verse in this section is a triumphant restatement of what Paul has been saying: "When Christ, who is your life, appears, then you also will appear with him in glory" (3:4). That gives us a further clarification of not only our victorious life but of Christ's final victory. The two belong together.

Christ is our life. In his Philippian letter Paul said: "For to me, to live is Christ" (Phil. 1:21). And to the Galatians he witnessed: "I have been crucified with Christ and I no longer live, but Christ lives in me. The life I live in the body, I live by faith in the Son of God, who loved me and gave himself for me. I do not set aside the grace of God, for if righteousness could be gained through the law [or any of the things we do to stuff meaning into life], Christ died for nothing!" (Gal. 2:20,21). The same conviction in Romans stirs a hallelujah chorus in us: "Now if we died with Christ, we believe that we will also live with him . . .

100

In the same way, count yourselves dead to sin but alive to God in Christ Jesus" (Rom. 6:8,11).

Christ's physical resurrection has enabled our spiritual resurrection. The vital uniqueness of each of us, the combination of our minds and hearts, is raised to a new level of experience and expression. Previously we were centered on ourselves and our self-determinism. Now we are centered on Christ. He is the uplifted Lord who draws us up to the new level of life in fellowship with Him. Our minds are given the gifts of wisdom, knowledge and faith; our emotions are infused with the fruit of His indwelling Spirit producing love, joy, peace, patience, kindness, goodness, faithfulness, gentleness and self-control. Our wills are fortified with His guidance and the desire to obey. We become like Christ!

A Faith That Overcomes

This is the faith that overcomes. When John wrote to the early Church, he wanted them to know that as long as life was focused on Christ the Christians could overcome the world. The word for "overcome" and "victory" come from the same Greek word *nikao*. "You, dear children, are from God and have overcome them [the world], because the one who is in you is greater than the one who is in the world . . . For everyone born of God has overcome the world. This is the victory that has overcome the world, even our faith. Who is it that overcomes the world? Only he who believes that Jesus is the Son of God" (1 John 4:4; 5:4,5). We have overcome the world when we lift our eyes from the things of earth and seek the things that are above. Then we can say, "Thanks be to God!

He gives us the victory through our Lord Jesus Christ" (1 Cor. 15:57).

The Final Victory

The victorious life is ultimately based on our conviction of the Lord's second coming. He will return in glory. History is not an endless stream of eventualities. There will be a final triumph of the Lord in His return. We live by an undiminishable hope: "When Christ . . . appears, then you also will appear with him in glory" (Col. 3:4). That's all we need to know. The end is sure, and in the meantime, Clement of Alexandria was right, "Christ turns all our sunsets into dawns."

Claiming the Victory

Some of us would have to admit that talk about the victorious life is disturbing. We believe in Christ's victory, but we don't feel very victorious. We know ourselves too well for that. There are thoughts, feelings, attitudes and habits which mock the reality of the victorious life in us. We are very aware of our impotence to change some of the things which still debilitate and defeat us. We are discouraged by our human nature.

We're not alone. The Colossian Christians had the same problem. In verses 5-11 Paul deals with the problems of defeated Christians. He helps us to realize that although the crucial battle has been fought and won through our death to self and resurrection to new life, the Holy Spirit must penetrate and occupy our total nature. Paul uses some very powerful imperatives to show us how. We are to put to death whatever belongs to our earthly nature, such as "sexual immorality, impurity, lust, evil desires and greed which is idolatry." He admonishes us to rid ourselves "of anger, malice, slander, filthy language." We are not to "lie to each other," since we have "taken off our old self with its practices, and have put on the new self which is [in the process of] being renewed in knowledge in the image of its Creator."

Read this section carefully. You may wish to substitute some of the words of your own particular hang-ups or expressions of the old nature. But be specific. That's the secret of claiming the victory. As we are honest with God about the things which separate us from Him and prompt us to misuse others, He can forgive each one and give us specific power over particular sins. List them out boldly! What are they for you?

The "wrath of God" Paul mentions is our hope. This is His penetrating love. He cares about us and wants to destroy those things which destroy our relationship with Him. Wrath is the other half of grace. The Lord will not wink with easy acceptance at those things which constantly cripple us. He works through the layers of our conscious and subconscious mind, excavating all of the vestiges of our self-centered nature. He's up to a great thing in us. He wants to recreate us in the image of His Son. One by one He forces us to deal with aspects of our old nature. Each one must be separately broken and put to death.

The victorious life is constant and continuous. The Lord is never finished with us. But we must cooperate; He will not force the new nature on us. The things which rob us of knowing and experiencing the victorious life must be surrendered to Him. The cycle of death and resurrection, commitment and liberation, is recapitulated over again with each aspect of our nature, attitudes and actions we entrust to Him.

If we don't feel victorious it's a sure sign we haven't claimed the power of Christ's victory for the specific things which rob us of joy and freedom. Before you turn this page or put this book down, ask yourself, "What is it that makes me feel defeated or discouraged about myself and my relationships?" Don't generalize. Be definite. Ask God to expose to you what got you locked on dead center. Then take them one by one and pray, "Gracious Lord, thank you for showing me what keeps me from the victorious life. I surrender it to you. I claim Christ's defeat of that on Calvary, and accept the same power which raised Him from the dead to be different. Thank you for living your life in me. I give you complete control to make me the person you want me to be."

That prayer is itself a victory. The victorious life is on the way. Claim it and thank God!

Life in Jesus' Style

+ + +

Colossians 3:12-17

There is a great deal of talk these days about life-style. The term is a new way of describing how we live out our basic convictions. Our life-style is the manner in which we relate to others, spend our time, and express our individuality. It's the characteristic mode of our communication and distinctive application of our values. Life-style is ethics, priorities, and acquired customs all rolled into observable behavior. We can usually tell what a person believes is important by his style of life.

Life in Jesus' style is life as He lived it and now lives it in us. He is both example and enabler of a quality of life. We begin to live in Jesus' style when we reproduce what we have received. He promised,

"I tell you the truth, anyone who has faith in me will do what I have been doing" (John 14:12). And then He gave us the power to fulfill the promise. "You will realize that I am in my Father, and you are in me, and I am in you" (John 14:20).

Paul took Jesus at His word. He was convinced that the living Christ resides in the minds and hearts of the Christians. The life, message, and indwelling power of the Lord is the motive and mandate of Christian living.

In Colossians 3:12-17, we have a beautiful ebb and flow between what the Lord has done and what we are to do. In this passage each example of the grace of God is coupled with a specific challenge. Constant reflection on the goodness of the Lord will produce consistent reproduction in our lives. The new kind of life we are to live is not one of compulsion, seeking to earn the Lord's approval, but one of conviction, allowing Him to express Himself through us. We have been called as His representatives, to act and react as He did, and to be to others what He has been to us in love, forgiveness, and encouragement.

Paul describes the Christian life-style in the vivid imagery of clothing. The admonition, "clothe yourselves," is the key to the whole passage. The Scriptures use this expression often. Jesus told His disciples they would be "clothed with power from on high" (Luke 24:49). Peter challenged the Christians to "clothe yourselves with humility toward one another" (1 Pet. 5:5). In the Old Testament the term means to be enveloped by a quality. In 2 Chronicles 6:41 the people are called to be "clothed with salvation," Job said God was clothed with "terrible majesty" (Job 37:22, *KJV*). The Psalmist said to God, "Thou art clothed with honor and majesty" (Ps. 104: 1, *KJV*); and described the wicked as clothed with cursing as his coat (see Ps. 109:18).

Building on this mode of expression, Paul admonishes the Colossians to put on the Saviour, to clothe themselves with Christ. In Ephesians and Thessalonians, he talks about putting on the armor of Christ and enumerates the Christian virtues. What he means in these passages, and here in Colossians, was that we are to become so possessed by the indwelling mind of Christ that our thoughts, feelings, expressions, and actions not only will resemble, but reproduce the life He lived and now lives in us. In this context we can consider the six motivations of what the Lord has done in us and the six mandates of what we are to do in the world. Each compelling couplet is an aspect of life in Jesus' style.

The Ethics of Election

In the first motivation of the Christian life Paul gets back to basics: "Therefore, as God's chosen people, holy and dearly loved" (Col. 3:12). Our ethics flow out of our election. We are chosen people, the elect of God. The Greek term means selected out of a number. We have been called to be God's people, not because of our goodness, but because of His grace. This results in praise, not pride. The overflowing gratitude for the call of God is what creates in us the desire to allow Him to guide and control our actions. Responsibility to emulate Christ is in response to the amazing love we have experienced. We are "holy and dearly loved." Holy means set apart. We have been singled out to be the recipients of profound love. Calvary is the focus of that love which knows no bounds. The tender words "dearly loved" are a translation of *agapao*, "beloved." We are the beloved of God, the cherished subjects of a love which is never calculated by our performance.

The experience of this love is the basis of the Christian style of life—the taproot. When we are constantly renewed with fresh discoveries of this love, we want to live in faithfulness and obedience. The same is true of human relationships. When we know we are loved and that love is not dependent on our adequacy or performance, we want to do everything we can to express our gratitude.

But when that affirming love is absent, we find it difficult to do what someone wants. Fear, guilt, or obligation are inadequate motivations. All of us have relationships like that. They result in frustration or a determined effort to please. Not so with our Lord! We desire to please Him because we know He is pleased with us already. What a difference!

The other day a new Christian said to me, "I can't get over it. The Lord's love is so different than the love I have received from my parents and friends. Their love is always a bargain and barter. It's not love at all; it's manipulation. I keep saying over and over, 'I belong to Christ. His love will never change. He loves me just as I am.' And you know, all I want to do is love Him in return and love people the way He has loved me!" My prayer for this new saint is that he will never lose that liberating motivation.

That was Paul's deepest desire for the Colossians. Love expressed in the Lord's call and election was the motivation to "clothe yourself with compassion, kindness, humility, gentleness and patience" (3:12). These are the characteristics of the character of Christ expressed through us.

The challenge is to let Christ reach out through us to others in the way He did to people in His earthly ministry. Compassion will be the first evidence of that. The word is a translated combination of heart and mercy. Christ in us produces a tenderhearted mercy. The meaning of mercy in Hebrew is to live in another's skin, to feel what he feels, to sense what he is going through. The test that we have experienced the true mercy of our Lord is that we become merciful. Our hearts are tenderized by His understanding and acceptance. Our judgments are softened and our icy negations are melted.

Kindness is mercy expressed in our disposition. It is grace in action; specific deeds and words which communicate the value and dignity of another person.

Humility enables this kindness. It puts the needs of others before our own. When we feel the Lord's love in spite of what we have been, we are broken open to care about others. True humility comes from the experience of the greatness of God and the realization that He has made us great by grace. There no longer is a need to prove ourselves by lording it over others. We are humble because we know that we could not think a thought, breathe a breath, or achieve anything worthwhile without Him. All that we have and are is but a reflection of Him. That cures arrogance and self-assertiveness.

Gentleness comes naturally from humility. The

word in the Greek is meekness, that inner realization of God's control which is expressed in sensitivity and empathy to others. When we are under God's control, we do not need to control others.

Patience caps off the list. Again it is the reproduction of what the Lord has done and is doing in us. The continuing experience of the limitless endurance of His love is the source of patience with others. When we think of the cross, all that our Lord has had to put up with in us, and how slow we have been to grow, we become patient with the people in our lives.

The Motive and Mandate of Forgiveness

The second dimension of the Christian life-style is forgiveness. Once again motive and mandate are inseparable: "Bear with each other and forgive whatever grievances you may have against one another. Forgive as the Lord forgave you" (3:13). The dynamic is the simultaneous experience of being forgiven and forgiving. There is a direct proportion between our acceptance of forgiveness and our capacity to forgive. Christ in us assures us that we are forgiven and gives us the power to forgive.

That leaves us with some disturbing questions. Is there anything in me that needs our Lord's forgiveness? Am I carrying the burden of guilt about any thought or action? New experiences of forgiveness make us forgiving people. Now we can ask: Is there anyone whom I need to forgive? Would the people around me recognize me as a forgiven and forgiving person? Are there any hurts I am harboring?

If Christ is our model and motivation, we need to remember three things about His forgiveness. *First,* it is given before we sin and before we ask to be forgiven; it is His consistent and persistent disposition toward us.

Secondly, the Lord's forgiveness is specific. He suffered on the cross for us. Our confession of a particular need for forgiveness is dealt with in the same grace. Each time we return seeking forgiveness, it is offered freely but with specific supplication. We know that we are forgiven for each separate sin.

Thirdly, the forgiveness of Christ is realized as a result of His overture to us. He breaks the barrier and comes to us. He does not wait.

That's the way He wants to forgive through us. He desires to make us people who are known for forgiveness which others realize is offered before they ask. The person of Christ in us can make forgiveness an undeniable part of our personality. But because people need to be assured of particularized forgiveness, we are to be people who sense the need in people and take the first step in reconciliation.

That's a big order! Who can live that way? Like Peter, we want to know the limits of forgiveness: "Lord, how many times shall I forgive my brother when he sins against me? Up to seven times?" The Lord's answer is disturbing: "I tell you, not seven times, but seventy-seven times" (Matt. 18:21,22). The Hebraism "seventy-seven" is also translated "seventy times seven," meaning without limit, on and on. Jesus' challenge was that there is never a point at which we can say, "I've gone far enough! I have fulfilled the requirement. I will forgive no more." Peter did not understand that until after the cross. It was then that he could comprehend the se-

111

cret of the Master's word: "He loves little who has been forgiven little" (Luke 7:47). The implied truth is that those who are loved deeply forgive freely. And that's exacly what He does in us. He loves and forgives. That gives us power to be forgiving people.

Paul knew this from his own experience. He called himself the chief of sinners. He could never dismiss the thought that Christ had loved and forgiven him all that he had done. His whole life was fired by the energy of that dominant conviction. When he challenged the Colossians to be forgiving he used a word which was a form of the word grace. The Greek word for grace, *charis*, is in the root of *charizomai*, "forgiveness." That grace was to be expressed for all the things the Colossian Christians had against each other and those beyond their fellowship. The depth and degree of the Lord's forgiveness was the inescapable standard. That little word "as" looms up in the sentence: "Forgive as the Lord forgave you." It means "according to, just as much as, in direct proportion, to the full degree."

That presses us to wonder: Could it be that the reason forgiving is so difficult is that we don't feel forgiven? If we are having problems forgiving, perhaps the thing we need is not to try harder, but to admit to our Lord that we desperately need His love for ourselves. Once that is real again, forgiveness will flow naturally.

This is what Paul means when He says, "And over all these virtues put on love, which binds them all together in perfect unity" (Col. 3:14). All the elements of the garment of Christ are sewn together by love. In a way, all the virtues are but manifestations of love and particular expressions of it. In his list of the fruit of the Spirit in Galatians 5:22, Paul puts love at the top of the list: "joy, peace, patience, kindness, goodness, faithfulness, gentleness and self-control" all are fruit from the root of love. The bond of love with Christ, the intimate union with Him, issues in all the other elements of a life in Jesus' style.

It took me a long time to learn this. In my Christian education as a boy I was given the impression that I should try by my own strength to be patient, kind, and faithful. That's where so many church school programs go wrong. We are led to believe that we are to honor Christ by living out the Christian virtues. Seldom is the mystery exposed that Christianity is impossible without a bond with Christ Himself. When I learned that the virtues are inadvertent, that they came from a relationship with the Saviour, I experienced the joy of Jesus' style. How I wish I had learned that earlier. The transferred life is the triumphant life.

In our morning worship services at Hollywood Presbyterian we often sing the folk-tune, "We Are One in the Bond of Love." At that time in the services we turn and greet the people around us. It helps us to realize that our individual bond with Christ has made us one with each other. Christianity is not a solo flight in a vertical ascent to God. It is a relationship with the Lord which immediately relates us to other believers and makes us responsible for them.

When Paul speaks of the perfect bond of love with Christ, his mind immediately leaps to the fellowship which is to be the provisional demonstration of all that God had in mind for His people from the beginning of Creation. The Lord is on the move not only calling new people into oneness with Him, but creating a new people, a new humanity, to duplicate individual oneness with Him with corporate oneness in the fellowship. He is equally concerned about the quality of our life together as a church as He is about the quality of our personal lives.

Peacemakers in Jesus' Style

Again, Paul couples source and semblance. The peace of Christ given to each of us is for the establishment of peace in the fellowship. This is the third dimension of life in Jesus' style. "Let the peace of Christ rule in your hearts, since, as members of one body, you were called to peace" (Col. 3:15). The word for rule comes from the athletic world. The meaning is "be umpire." It is the word used for an umpire who makes decisions on matters of dispute or priority. Just as an umpire settles questions in an athletic event, so peace is the deciding factor in all personal and interpersonal affairs in the Christian life.

The peace of Christ is first the umpire of the individual heart. It forces us to evaluate all attitudes and actions on the basis of whether they will maintain peace in our own lives. There are things we are tempted to do and say which will create turmoil in our inner being. The umpire of peace overrules those temptations. We can ask our Lord, "If I do this will it rob me of peace?" Or, "If I continue to express these emotions, will I have peace of soul?"

The same basic qualification is for the relationships of the church. The meaning of the word peace is to

114

"bind together, unify into integrated oneness." The peace of the church is crucial to our Lord. Therefore, we can allow Him to be the arbiter of differences. Christian relationships are never direct; they are always through Christ. The Christ in us relates to the Christ in another. The challenge is to seek what Christ wants and wills. That brings a loving fellowship moving in the same direction.

Yet, we are all honest to admit that some of our most excruciating differences have come with other Christians. Good men and women do not always agree. Churches are often in turmoil and conflict over customs, procedures and priorities. I find that the only hope for the church to be an example of unity to the world is in seeking the mind of Christ together.

I find the following questions a good inventory to seek the will of Christ and keep His peace:

1. What does the Lord want us to do?

2. If we did it would it be in keeping with His life, message and guidance?

3. Would the anticipated action or program glorify Christ? Would He do it if He were in charge? (He is, though we often forget that He is!)

4. Is it in keeping with the message of Scripture, the Word of God, our only rule for faith and practice?

5. Will it bring us closer to Him and each other?

There are times when our Lord, through our study of Scripture, leads us to question, contradict, and change customs and practices which have been cherished for years. But we must be sure that our authority and motive of the change are the Lord's and not our lust for innovation.

True peace can be known only between those

whose hearts are controlled by the peace of Christ. Christian peace is much more than a lack of conflict or hostility. We all long for peace in our world. That will never happen until it is based on the peace of Christ, and that will never be established in treaties or a balance of power. True peace begins in the believer, is shared between those who want Christ's will above their own desires, and then spreads out into a community, nation and the world.

What about your church and mine? Would the people in our towns say that peace is a powerful sign of the lordship of Christ in our churches? What does the Lord have to say to each of us about the next steps of becoming a peacemaker? Not peace at any price, but peace at the highest price of seeking His will and doing it together.

The Guidance of the Gift of Wisdom

But peace is dependent on another of the gifts of our Lord's indwelling presence: the guidance of the wisdom of God. Paul knew that peace could not come in the Colossian church without this fourth aspect of Christian life-style. "Let the word of Christ dwell in you richly as you teach and counsel one another with all wisdom" (3:16).

In Colosse, where the Gnostics claimed a secret wisdom, Paul reminded the Christians that they had the wisdom about the very nature of God and His plan for life revealed in Jesus Christ. The "word of Christ" is a synonym for His living presence in us revealing and integrating His message and direction. When that word dwells in us richly we become the recipients not only of the meaning of his truth proclaimed in His ministry, but the impact of His own specific situational guidance.

We have met that word "dwell" before. The fullness of God dwelt in Jesus. Now the fullness of Christ dwells in us. The word for dwell, remember, is from *oikos*, meaning "at home." Its form here implies "to live in a house at home." The Lord is at home in our hearts and minds. All the wisdom of the Lord is ours as a result. But Paul goes on. The Word dwells "richly," meaning abundantly, without any limitation, fully, and completely. He communicates to us from within about the deepest secrets of life and guides our every word and action.

This gives us our capacity to "teach and counsel one another with all wisdom." We become communicators of the Lord to one another. The words "teach and counsel" belong together. One is conceptual, the other is relational. We present the truth, but stand with a person with undiminishable loyalty and patience to help him act on that truth. The word "counsel" has been translated as both admonish and exhort. It carries the deeper meaning of enabling a person to see what the Lord is saying to him and then assisting him to appropriate what he sees.

A crucial part of the Christian life-style is our becoming a contagious communicator. Those of us in whom Christ lives neither stand by while others are troubled nor wring our hands in desperation. We become responsible for the people around us. All that happens to them is our concern. We are to pray to understand, ask the Lord for the words to speak, and dare to lay our lives alongside those in trouble if we are to be the love of our Lord to them. Christ never gives us wisdom for intellectual word games or to impress others. He gives His gift for costly ministry.

A Life of Thanksgiving

A fifth element of life in Jesus' style is thanksgiving. You may wonder how gratitude is a part of a style of life. It is the key which unlocks our potential and makes us receptive to more of the Lord's power. Praise and adoration expressed in thanksgiving open the floodgates of the Spirit. The more we give thanks, the more we can receive.

A person in Christ comes to learn that thanksgiving not only gives praise for the pleasures of life but also the problems. Thanksgiving heals pride and opens the door to the Lord's blessing in difficulty. When things are going well and we give thanks, we acknowledge that all of life is a gift; but more so in anguishing perplexity. Paul said: "Give thanks in all circumstances, for this is God's will for you in Christ Jesus" (1 Thess. 5:18). The very moment we can thank God for a problem, or an excruciating person or situation, we become open to receive the help the Lord is ready to give. He can bless a thankful person because his heart is open and receptive.

A woman who has faced physical infirmities expressed the dynamics of thanksgiving to God, "I was resentful and hostile that this thing happened to me. I could see no reason for it. Then a friend helped me to thank God for what could happen in me through what was happening to me. My recovery began in that moment of gratitude. God had been ready long before to help and heal me. It was as if my thanksgiving was a final surrender and acceptance."

A man said the same thing about some difficulties in his marriage. "When I thanked God that He was at work in us in spite of our problems, I felt release and freedom. I know that the long process of reconciliation began when I could praise God—not that He sent the difficulty, but that He would use it to bring us to a new life together."

A young man facing uncertainties about the future was able to thank God for the valley of indecision.

A pastor thanked God for a tradition-bound church and that broke him free to lead his people to freedom.

Again, what is true for individuals is also true for the church. The Colossian Christians faced impossible odds. Paul challenged them to become a singing church "as you sing psalms, hymns and spiritual songs with gratitude in your hearts to God" (Col. 3:16). He knew that if the church could sing the Psalter and the Scriptures, along with some of the new hymns common among believers even at that early stage of the development of Christianity, it would not be long before assurance and hope would be reborn.

Recently, I was asked to contribute a list of my 10 favorite hymns to a compiler of a new hymnal. I submitted these as hymns which had sustained and strengthened me in so many times of need:

"Amazing Grace"
"Guide Me, O Thou Great Jehovah"
"Beneath the Cross of Jesus"
"Crown Him with Many Crowns"
"Joyful, Joyful, We Adore Thee"

"Praise Ye the Lord, the Almighty,
   The King of Creation"
"The Lord Is My Shepherd" (Crimmond)
"O for a Thousand Tongues to Sing"
"How Great Thou Art"
"Jesus, Jesus, There Is Something
   About That Name"
"Holy, Holy" (Jimmy Owens)
"To God Be the Glory,
   Great Things He Has Done"
"Because He Lives" (Gaither)

As I made up the list, I realized how much these hymns had meant to me in times of frustration. I can vividly remember how much William Cowper's hymn meant to me at a time of spiritual peril:

God moves in a mysterious way
His wonders to perform;
He plants His footsteps in the sea,
And rides upon the storm.
Deep in unfathomable mines
Of never-failing skill
He treasures up His bright designs,
And works His sovereign will.

And many times at memorial services I have sung Luther's "A Mighty Fortress Is Our God" with families with whom I had shared the loss of a loved one. Hymns of trust and confidence unbind the frustrated or grieving heart to thank and praise God.

Karl Barth once said, "A church which has no great anguish on its heart will have no great music on its lips." The Psalter and the hymnbook are wonderful resources for daily devotions. Also, it's uplifting to take a portion of Scripture from the New Testament and sing its words with joy as the spontaneous music flows from a thankful heart.

Life in the Power of Jesus' Name

The sixth and final aspect of the Christian style of life given us by the Apostle is that the ultimate source of power and direction for the Christian is the name of Jesus Christ. "And whatever you do, whether in word or deed, do it all in the name of the Lord Jesus, giving thanks to God the Father through him" (3:17). That summarizes and crowns all the rest. Jesus' name is the source of the Christian's authority and power—the promise of His victory.

The name of Jesus unleashes the power of God. His name is above any name. To pray in Jesus' name is to penetrate to the heart of God. It is also the litmus test of the authenticity of our prayers. If we can ask in Jesus' name, it must be in keeping with His message and life. When it is, we can be assured of the same power revealed by Him.

The Christian is one whose style is reflective of the immense resources of God at work in him. His life is punctuated by the exclamation points of the amazing interventions of God. He is bold and free, unafraid and courageous, because he knows that nothing can separate him from the source of his power. Therefore, he lives an astounding life in which the impossible happens.

Paul has given the Colossians what they needed; a picture of what Christ could do in them. He knew that if they saw His potential and not just their problems, they would dare to live with delight and abandonment. That's what we all need. A new focus, a liberating image for our imagination. Life in Jesus' style is nothing other than Jesus living His life today in you and me.

LIFE-STYLE INVENTORY

It is helpful to ask ourselves penetrating questions about the extent that the realization of the truth of the gospel and the experience of the living, indwelling Christ have had on our character and life-style. In Colossians 3:12-17, Paul has given affirmations of the love of God and admonitions of how to express it in our relationships. You may wish to evaluate the extent to which you have received what God offers, and the depth to which you have expressed what you have received in actual, living practice.

We will consider the motive and the mandate of Christian living. On a scale of one to ten, rate the level of your receptivity under Part I, and the degree of your reproduction under Part II. Total each section. The degree of difference between the total of Part I with Part II will help you discern the relationship between what you believe and what you are living out in daily experience.

Part I   The Motive of the Christian Life

_____ A. I realize I have been chosen by God. I belong to Him.

_____ B. I have received the gift of a new life in Christ. That new life began when I received His indwelling life in me.

_____ C. I know His deep love and concern for me.

_____ D. I have let God forgive me and heal my memories of the past.

____ E. I have received and feel the peace of Christ.

____ F. I have found the message of Christ to be the answer to my questions and the basis of my understanding of life, death and eternal hope.

____ G. Thanksgiving for all the Lord has done and given fills me with awe, gratitude and new openness to Him for the future.

____ Total of our receptivity

Part II   The Mandate of Christian Living

The extent to which our receptivity has equaled reproductive responsibility in our life-style as a representative of Christ.

____ A. I feel a tender-hearted mercy and kindness toward the people of my life.

____ B. I am free of the necessity of making a good impression. I can be authentically myself without projecting an image.

____ C. I am able to suffer quietly and patiently with others without demanding recognition and reward.

____ D. I am gentle in judgments and ready to forgive.

____ E. Love is the dominant guide for what I say and do.

____ F. I am able to express the peace of Christ I have experienced by being a peacemaker with and between others.

____ G. The people around me are aware that I am thankful for the gift of life; sense that I am delighted to be me; know that I acknowledge with praise all I have and am has come from our Lord; feel my appreciation for them; witness my gratitude as my key to facing life's problems.

_____ *Total of our reproductive responsibility*
_____ *Difference between total of Part I and Part II*

The Relational Gospel

+ + +

Colossians 3:18—4:1

The gospel is relational. It declares a dramatic, new way to live in our relationships with God and one another. We are related to God by the grace of Christ's death and resurrection. Through His indwelling power we have been enabled to reproduce that grace in our love, forgiveness and acceptance of others. The test of our relationship with God will be in the relationships we have with people.

In Colossians 3:18–4:1, Paul spells out the relational gospel for marriage, our family and our vocation. These three spheres of human relationships are where most of us need to grow. People are problems for all of us. At the center of most difficulties there are difficult people. Conflict is rooted in the difference between people's values and agenda. Our backgrounds and experience often cause us to want people to perform according to our standards. We all need to be loved but the way we express our need sometimes makes us very unlovable.

What can we do about our relationships? How can we communicate love in meaningful ways? What should we do with our own unsatisfied needs when people disappoint us? Paul answers these questions in this section of Colossians. His language and expressions need to be understood in the context of the time in which he wrote, but what he said is still a reliable guide for remedial relationships.

Relationships in Marriage

Paul's admonitions to husbands and wives about the marriage relationship must be considered both in the light of his other epistles and the conditions of marriage then.

Before we do our exposition on what he had to say to wives and husbands, it is helpful to turn to Ephesians 5, with an eye on a crucial passage in 1 Corinthians 7.

In Ephesians, Paul precedes his advice to married people with powerful preparation. Ephesians 5:1-31 has some challenges which give contextual light on what he will say about marriage: "Be imitators of God, therefore, as dearly loved children and live a life of love, just as Christ loved us and gave himself up for us as a fragrant offering and sacrifice of God" (Eph. 5:1). He then challenges them to live as new people, free of sexual immorality, impurity or greed. Christians are to live in the light of the Lord with all relationships open to honesty and integrity. He cautions about the power of evil and then counsels the Ephesians: "Sing and make music in your heart to the Lord" (v. 19).

The key for understanding Christian marriage follows: "always giving thanks to God the Father for *everything*, in the name of our Lord Jesus Christ. Submit to one another out of reverence for Christ" (vv. 20,21, italics added). Marriage is to be evaluated as part of the "everything" that is to be done in the name of the Lord. Our first commitment is to Him. That is the essential relationship. Until we are one with Him we cannot be one in marriage. If our need to be loved is not satisfied by Christ we will not be able to love a mate creatively.

As thankful people, we are to submit to one another out of reverence for Christ. This is a fundamental ingredient in all Christian relationships. The life filled with the Holy Spirit is free to submit to others in the fellowship. In the Greek word for submit, *hupotasso*, the verb *tasso* means "to marshall troops or armaments" in order for battle or array under a commander; *hupo*, the prefixed preposition, means "under." Thus hupotasso means to put under the leadership of, or be in subjection to, a leader. A Christian is one who can be led by Christ along with his fellow believers for the good of all. Our lives are not to be marked by blistering independence and self-will but willingness to be guided for the accomplishment of a task. We do this out of reverence for Christ. All Christians, and especially *both* husbands and wives, are to express the quality of natural subjection out of love and honor to Christ.

In 1 Corinthians 7, Paul further affirms the mutuality of the marriage bond.. "Each man should have his own wife, and each woman her own husband" (7:2). Now don't miss the impact of the next sentences. "The husband should fulfill his marital duty to his wife, and likewise the wife to her husband. The wife's body does not belong to her alone but also to her husband. In the same way, the husband's body does not belong to him alone but also to his wife" (7:3,4).

From this passage we draw the obvious conclusion that Paul believed in the shared responsibility of men and women in marriage. He proclaimed the great new Christian marriage commandment of mutual subjection and submissive willingness to give ourselves to one another in gratitude to Christ.

Paul often has been criticized as one who was down on women. Actually, he presented a radically new view of marriage which elevated women to a position of equality in marriage. When we look at marriage in both the Hebrew and Roman societies of Paul's time, we realize what a dramatically different concept of life together in marriage he presented. As a rabbi and Pharisee he probably was taught the prayer, "I thank thee, God, that I was not born a woman." The Jewish attitude toward divorce exposes the attitude toward women and marriage at that time. A man could change wives easily and with little justification. The annotated rules and regulations of the scribes outlined all of the reasons a man had the right to divorce his wife, but gave no help in establishing a truly great marriage. The Gentile attitude toward marriage was no better. Women were related to as "things" to be used and enjoyed, not loved and cherished. They were viewed as totally subservient to men in the home and society. It was a man's world in every way. Women were not recognized as capable of intelligence, leadership or creativity.

Jesus' attitude toward women and marriage was revolutionary. He treated women as persons, not as playthings for gratification or as the necessary agents of procreation. When the Pharisees wanted to draw Him into disputation about divorce, He forced them back to a confrontation with God's original and eternal intention for marriage: "Some Pharisees came and tested him by asking, 'Is it lawful for a man to divorce his wife?'

" 'What did Moses command you?' he replied.

"They said, 'Moses permitted a man to write a certificate of divorce and send her away.'

" 'It is because your hearts were hard that Moses wrote you this law,' " Jesus replied. " 'But at the beginning of creation, God "made them male and female. For this reason a man will leave his father and mother and be united to his wife, and the two will become one flesh." So they are no longer two, but one. Therefore what God has joined together, let man not separate!' " (Mark 10:2-9).

A new teaching, indeed! In private with His disciples, Jesus declared that anyone who divorces his wife because of his desire for another woman, commits adultery. Marriage and the family were part of God's plan for His people. The bonds were sacred and holy.

Paul spelled out the implications of the Lord's message in his teaching to the early church. In the light of distortions of marriage in both the Hebrew and Gentile mind, we can appreciate what a task of communication he had. He did not demean the role of women. Quite the contrary, his teaching was a strategic step forward toward the recovery of God's original dignity of persons.

With this background, Paul's message to the Colossians about the role of men and women is very exciting. The essential quality he singled out for each was to be expressed by both.

"Wives, submit to your husbands, as is fitting in the Lord" (Col. 3:18). The same word for submit used in Ephesians is repeated here—*hupotasso*, to put yourself under the leadership of another. Paul wanted all Christians to express this quality. The wives were the first group to be given it as a particularized challenge. They were to lead the way in bringing this dynamic quality to marriage. Not because they were inferior but because they were to be initiators of mutual submission.

The Apostle's word to wives is not a delegation to a lesser position. Actually, I interpret it as elevation. Submissiveness is a necessary basis of any great marriage. I believe that God has given women a very special gift to model the power of victory through surrender. But it is no less the responsibility of the husband. Bristled individualism and aggressive independence must be replaced by mutual submission to each other.

Who's in Charge Here?

The battle for control frustrates most marriages. "Who's in charge here?" is a question which troubles many marriages. It's a distracting question which leads us away from the central issue. Christ is the head of a Christian marriage. He's in charge. When a husband and wife have both submitted to His lordship they can be submissive to receive His guidance and wisdom through each other. The husband is not the only one of the two who has access to the Lord in prayer. Submission is not giving in to the conquering force of another. It is the willing commitment to receive openly what another person has to offer. We become creatively submissive in marriage when we are open to listen, free to give ourselves to another's need, receptive to his or her values and visions. Two heads are not better than one unless both have been made one in Christ as the head of the house.

Of course, any unit of society needs a leader. When Christ is the acknowledged leader of a marriage, then the husband can become a sensitive leader of his home. But any creative leader learns the secret that people can support only what they share in developing. He will listen to those he leads and allow them to shape the strategy for accomplishing agreed-upon goals. Leadership in a marriage is not a solo flight to the Lord for direction and back again with imperious authority. A submissive wife's slogan is not, "Whatever you say, dear!" as if the Lord never said anything to her.

The meaning of the Greek word for submit carries the implication of entrusting oneself to the leadership of another to accomplish a task. When both husband and wife submit to seek the mind of Christ together, He will guide their decisions together. Their wills will be one to discover and do the will of the Lord.

The Lord gives us all different gifts. For a woman to be unable to contribute her gifts because she is a woman is absurd. God brings people together to complement and help each other. It is a sad situation when a husband feels that he must have all the gifts of wisdom, knowledge and insight. Authentic leadership from a husband should be given after he has prayed both alone and with his wife. There is a great difference between saying, "Do what I say—I'm in charge here!" and "It seems to me that from our prayers and the guidance we both feel that this is what we should do."

Paul's exhortation to the husbands at Colosse was that they should love their wives and not be harsh with them. The word for love that is used is *agape*, the love revealed by Jesus Christ on the cross.

That love is born in the heart of one who accepts Christ as Lord and Saviour. It is more than affection, *philio*, which is dependent on the adequacy or attractiveness of the recipient. A husband has the right to be the leader of his home when his heart and attitude are filled with Christ's love.

In Ephesians Paul clarified the necessity of the leadership of the husband. "For the husband is the head of the wife as Christ is the head of the church, his body, of which he is the Saviour. Now as the church submits to Christ, so also wives should submit to their husbands in everything" (Eph. 5:23,24).

That says more about the quality of the husband's leadership than the wife's submission. The Church submits to Christ as Head of the Body because of His love, forgiveness and compassion. Christ's credentials for leadership were a cross and unlimited grace. He laid down His life for those He led. His right to lead was in the absolute reliability of His care. Any man who emulates Christ will be worthy of the submission of his wife.

I have never talked to a woman who would not be willing to be led by a husband who loved her as Christ loved the Church as its Head. Christ gave us the secret of leadership and submission. He sublimely revealed both qualities in His life. He was submissive to God and the needs of the people. He went to the cross out of obedience to God and to provide a way of reconciliation for those whom He loved so profoundly.

Paul says that this quality of love in a husband will keep him from being harsh. The word is *pikraino*, which means "irritation, embitterment and exasperation." The husband who is filled with Christ's indwelling Spirit will give leadership which does not cause the wife to feel left out, disqualified and unrespected. Harshness is the result of an insecurity in any leader. It indicates that the only way he can get his will done is by force, threats, coercion or bartered rewards.

A husband who has allowed Christ to control his attitudes and disposition is able to lead with tenderness, gentleness and sensitivity. His wife's needs are his persistent concern. Because he has submitted to Christ, he can submit to be the Lord's person to her. He becomes flexible and viable in seeking words and ways of love which will encourage and enable her. She will be cared for as a gift of God, not as his possession.

Children and Parents as Fellow Believers

Now Paul turns his attention to the family. The

context is still mutual acceptance and submission, a part of doing "all in the name of the Lord Jesus, giving thanks to God the Father through him" (Col. 3:17). Parents and children in the Christian family are to relate to each other in and through Christ.

The challenge Paul gives first to the children and then to the fathers is in the light of the fact that both groups belong to Christ and therefore have a unique quality of relationship with each other. What he asks them to do and be to each other is because of what Christ has been to them: "Children, obey your parents in everything, for this pleases the Lord" (3:20).

Obedience is the key to unlock the power of our relationship with the Lord Himself. There is no abundant life without it. To seek to know God's will and do it is the secret of joy. But obedience is based on our belief in the omniscience and all-pervading love of God. We can trust and obey Him because we know that He is for us and not against us; that He wills our ultimate good and will do everything to enable it; and that He knows our needs and will meet them in a way that will enable us to become the mature people He wants us to be.

Obedience by children to their parents should be based on the same quality of trust. Paul has a great deal to say about the kind of fathers who would be worthy of obedience from their children: "Fathers, do not embitter your children, or they will become discouraged" (3:21). The word embitter, *erethizo*, means "provoke or irritate." The word discouraged is *athumeo*, "to be disheartened, have your spirit broken, lose heart."

A parent's relationship with a child determines the

shape of his personality and all his future relationships with himself and others. Paul's concern is that a child can receive so little self-esteem that he will become discouraged about himself and his potential. Often a parent's own lack of self-acceptance is projected in unreasonable demands on his child. The inalienable right of every child of a Christian family is to experience delight and joy about himself from his parents. In the context of affirming love a child can and will obey. Disobedience is usually the result of lack of love.

A Christ-filled parent can prayerfully guide his child and lovingly expect follow-through on his direction. Discipline is an expression of love. It shows we care enough to want a child to grow. That concern gets through to a child and becomes the motivation for wanting to do what he knows his parents want.

I believe that as children grow, they need to know our own struggles and frustrations. As long as we must always have the complete answer for everything and have ourselves put together in every way (which can never be true), we give our children an unrealistic view of adulthood. It also discourages their own efforts to try, experience failure, and begin again.

Here's an inventory I take constantly and have taken with thousands of parents over the years.

1. Do I believe that my children are not mine but a gift from God entrusted to me?

2. Have I surrendered them and their future to the Lord? Do I feel that I am a copartner with God in enabling them to be the men and women He intended?

3. Do they know how delighted and excited I am

about them? Do they feel that my love is in no way conditioned by their performance? Do they feel that I am on their side, standing with them and for them in their problems and struggles?

4. Am I living a life in Christ that I would want them to emulate and reproduce? Do they know what Christ means to me? Have I shared the joy as well as the challenges of being Christ's person?

5. Is my corrective guidance and discipline creative? Is there authentic love in my efforts to demand and encourage follow-through on life's responsibilities?

6. Is there any insecurity or uneasy ambition in me that I am projecting onto my children? Can I release them to be what God wants according to His timing and priorities?

The thing that Paul wanted the children and parents of the Colossian church to discover was a mutual trust rooted in their shared faith in Christ. If these fathers followed his admonition, the children of those fathers would be able to please the Lord by obeying.

One of the most exciting things which I have experienced in my life in Christ is to discover my children as fellow disciples. When a child becomes a friend in Christ, it is an inexpressible joy. To be able to share my hopes and hurts with children, and pray with them, is a wonderful satisfaction. They often have insight and incisive understanding beyond my own. I have found that my receptivity to them, and to Christ through them, has provided an ambience in which I can share my hopes and dreams for them— more than parental advice—the shared vision of fellow adventurers!

Relationships in Our Work

This next section of Paul's relational message deals with people who work for us or for whom we work. He uses terms which are foreign to us, thank God! Our problem is not "slaves and masters." Paul was concerned about how Christian slaves related to pagan masters, but also how Christian masters treated their slaves. What can this section possibly have to say to us today? A great deal. All we have to do is interchange the words employer and employee for master and slave.

The person in Christ is to be distinguished for his conscientious, industrious integrity. The Lord is our true Master. We are to do our work as if we were working for Him. Some years ago, I had an assistant who worked harder than any pastor I have ever known. He was tireless in his efforts to do everything I suggested, and then so much more beyond. One day I said to him in appreciation, "I am deeply gratified by how hard you work for me."

He smiled and then said, "Thanks for saying that. But you know, I really am not doing it for you, but for the Lord!" Paul would have liked that answer.

When our work is done "as to the Lord" (Col. 3:22, *KJV*), it takes on a new perspective, but also a new excellence. At the end of each day or project, we should be able to say, "Lord, I've done my best because I did it for you." We have no other purpose than to please the Lord.

But that's not always true. Remuneration, recognition, false pride, competitiveness and compulsion often are our motives. We need to ask, "Why am I doing what I do?" The fact is that we were never meant to find meaning in our work but bring meaning to our work. When Christ is our meaning we can work creatively to praise Him. When our work becomes too important we make it a false god. That can be true whether we work on an assembly line or in the pulpit. Some of us have confused our self-worth with overwork. We feel urged to justify ourselves with our performance. True freedom in our employment comes when we seek the Lord's guidance about where to work, ask Him for His strength to work industriously and effectively, and leave the results of our success to Him.

When we place ourselves under the leadership of an employer we are to be obedient to that person as an act of faithfulness to Christ. Paul admonishes us to work hard not just when we are being watched or to win favor, but "with sincerity of heart and reverence for the Lord. Whatever you do, work at it with all your heart, as working for the Lord, not for men, since you know that you will receive an inheritance from the Lord as a reward. It is the Lord Christ you are serving" (3:22-24).

There are times when it's difficult to work for people whose purposes and goals, along with their policies and practices, contradict our convictions. Often our prayers lead us to change employment. But not before we have done all we can to share Christ and what He means to us with the people for whom we work. I believe that the Lord plants us in these very places where the gospel is needed most. Our reason for being there is not just the job, but what the Lord wants to have happen to the people around us.

I know a young lawyer who has claimed the floor

of the office building in which he works for Christ. The Lord has put him into contact with many people who need faith and hope.

A woman who works in a department store said, "I couldn't take working in here if it weren't for the chance to pray for the people I wait on."

An insurance man sees his work with people as an opportunity to share Christ's eternal life policy. So it goes. Saints in the marketplace, alive in Christ and using the relationships at work to spread the gospel.

A Word to Employers

Paul has a final word in this section to the masters. He is writing to Christians who own slaves. What he has to say is applicable to anyone who has people working for him. The key is that we are to relate to people in our employ as our Lord has related to us. Again the theme of this whole section is a new focus: "Masters, provide your slaves with what is right and fair, because you know that you also have a Master in heaven" (4:1).

Think of all the economic and business problems that would be solved if employers who are Christians lived out their faith in their businesses! Consider some of the industrial conflicts which have torn cities and nations apart because the Christian faith did not pervade the decisions of Christian industrialists. But that's easy historical retrospect.

The real question is how you and I relate to people who work with us or for us right now. Do we pray for them? Are they part of our visions for the business we share? Are they aware of our concern for what is "right and fair" for them? Do they know that because of Christ's love for us we are seeking to run our business, or group, or committee under the management of the Master?

Paul has led us through a penetrating reevaluation of our relationships. What he has said has implications for all the people of our lives. People are the first item on God's agenda. It's what happens in our relationships that counts. We have been given a relationship with Him to transform all other relationships. Christianity is not theoretical, it's relational.

Making the Most of Every Opportunity

+ + +

Colossians 4:2-6

Recently, in preparation for a conference in a church in the Middle West, I asked the church officers to write out their deepest hope for themselves and their church. The response of the elders, deacons and trustees of this prominent church all said the same thing in different ways. Their hope for themselves was that they could find the excitement of the new life in Christ and that their church would be filled with warmth and joy.

I hear the same longing in clergy at conferences called to find ways of renewing the local congregation. "How can we set our people on fire for Christ?" the pastors ask. "What can we do to recover the ebullient joy of New Testament Christianity in our time? Is there some program, some technique, a strategy we're missing?" Before the conferences go very far we are usually up against the reality that something must happen to us before it can happen to our congregations. The need is universal among clergy, church officers and millions of church people. The fire has gone out, the enthusiasm has gone dull, boredom with churchmanship has set in.

Why? How can so many good Christians feel the way they do with what they believe? How did they get that way? What banked the fires for a long hiatus of mediocrity? Is it the exhaustion from endless committee meetings, lifeless worship services, and irrelevant preaching?

The Division of Faith from Life

I think I have discovered an answer. We have divided faith from life. It's possible to believe in Christ, be a participant in church activities and support fine causes and miss the most obvious. The immediacy of the Lord is impinging on every situation. Intimacy with Him is discovered in opening all of life to Him and being amazed at what He can do with the people and problems of life.

We have arrived at a strange state of self-sufficiency in contemporary Christianity. We have organized out the possibility of Christ's surprising intervention. Our churches are filled with humanly adequate people who can handle daily living rather effectively. Prayer for Christ's power is reserved for big crises and momentous tasks. We don't need Him, we think, for our daily living.

In our churches, we talk about grand ideas of salvation, faith and grace. We seldom see the implications for marriage, the family, the loneliness of being single, the pressures on the job, difficult people and knotty complexities. Christ is off dealing with world problems; we should be mature enough to handle the

142

rest ourselves. But most serious of all, we don't catch the momentous power available to maximize the mundane and sensitize life with the presence of Christ. Separating our living from our relationship with Christ eventually results in a bland and boring Christianity.

The way back to an exciting Christian life is to live in momentary companionship with Christ, surrender all of our relationships and responsibilities to Him as we go through the days, and discover the missed potential every person and problem has to offer. Christ is the mighty maximizer. He can take every hour and energize it with unexpected, unforeseen, uncalculated happenings. The joy comes from seeing Him at work. When we begin to share this truth with one another, there'll be a change in our churches. Our experience of the Saviour will be updated daily and hourly with evidences of His power.

The Key to Discovering an Exciting Life

I am convinced that living in momentary companionship with Christ is what made Paul the magnetic person he was. From the time of his conversion, he was a man on the move for the Master. Every person was a potential convert to Christ; every complexity a new chance to trust the Saviour. He was intrepidly bold in danger and conflict. What did he have to lose? He belonged to Christ! In rejection and trial, he sought what Christ was trying to tell him in the circumstance. When he enjoyed success and triumph, he was filled with praise that the Saviour had used him.

The inner secret of Paul's relationship with Christ

is revealed in this next section of Colossians. In Colossians 4:2-6, we feel the importunity of his prayers to be effective right up to the end of his life.

The other day a man told me that most everyone has a word or phrase which exposes his meaning and purpose. This section contains Paul's: "Make the most of every opportunity" (4:5). That's it! There's Paul's heart for Christ. Imagine it. There he is chained to the guard in his quarters in Rome and the prayer he wanted the Colossians to pray for him and for themselves was that they would make the most of every opportunity.

Buying Up the Time

The Greek words of the text are fascinating: *ton kairon exagorazomenoi*. The verb means "to buy up an opportunity for one's self, to use everything and see everyone as an advantageous opportunity." The familiar translation is "redeeming the time." The word for time is *kairos*, "the strategic, crucial moment." *The New International Version* is not only faithful to the Greek but very helpful. We are to make the most of every opportunity.

That's exactly what Paul desired—that his friends in far off Colosse pray for him. What a gentle way of reminding them of the thing they needed—to pray for themselves: "Devote yourselves to prayer, being watchful and thankful" (4:2); continue steadfastly, watching. Paul wanted them to do both simultaneously.

Pray with your eyes wide open to the opportunities God will provide in answer to your prayers! Don't divide prayer and life. Keep them together and see what God can do with a ready and willing disciple.

Paul helps us to find the irreplaceable dynamic of exciting Christian living: to pray without ceasing; to expect amazing things from God and thank Him constantly. What a delightful way to live!

When Paul asked the Colossians to pray for an open door, "so that we may proclaim the mystery of Christ, for which I am in chains" (4:3), he wanted to be maximum for the Saviour in his imprisonment. But what Colossian Christian could pray that for Paul without wondering what doors of opportunity the Lord had standing wide open in Colosse?

I have a friend who has a way of asking me to pray for him the very things I need in my own life. His vulnerability engenders honesty about my own missed opportunities.

Paul was in chains. The Colossians, though they had problems, were free. How much more should they be aware of the potential of what God was about to do in, around and through them.

When the Apostle asked that they pray that he may proclaim the gospel freely as he should, his humility and desire to grow in effectiveness are exposed. He never felt that he had arrived or that he had learned all that the Saviour had to teach him. He wanted to find ways of getting through to the guards who were chained to him around the clock. He had not been as effective with the Jewish leaders in Rome as he had wished. The opportunity of Roman citizens visiting him was a great chance to share the gospel.

Kairos Time

The point for us is that every day and hour is filled

with *kairos* times. The Lord wants to make us ready for those whom He has made ready. There will be little excitement or fulfillment in our Christian living until we expect and claim the Lord's power to use us to help people we meet to know Him. Next to knowing Christ ourselves, the greatest joy is introducing others to Him. Our churches will not "come alive" until that's the daily vocation of church members.

Creative Conversation

And Paul tells us how: "Let your conversation be always full of grace, seasoned with salt, so that you may know how to answer everyone" (4:6). The suggestion is not to give advice, preach at people or harangue them with our favorite jargon. Conversation—daily exchange with people—is filled with opportunities to witness. If our conversation is to be a channel of witness, Paul says, it should be "full of grace" and "seasoned with salt."

To be full of grace—gracious—is to be warm, concerned, attentive to people's needs, courteous—these are implied. Grace is an outward expression of our realization of God's limitless, unchanging love.

There are Christians who have the gift of making others feel important and valued when they are with them. Other people open up like flower buds in the presence of the morning sun.

Salty Christians

Paul also suggests that our conversation be "seasoned with salt." I like that! Wit and humor—the zest of our own humanity filled with the laughter and sparkle of the Saviour. Salt is a preservative and seasoning. Our conversation should preserve the dignity and uniqueness of each person in his hopes and struggles and should bring out the best in him, like salt does in food. Our conversation should be seasoned—punctuated with personal illustrations of what the Saviour has done in our personal needs and complexities; a testimony to our identification with our Saviour.

Conversation that has these two qualities will enable us to "know how to answer everyone." Each person with whom we converse has his own set of peculiarities and possibilities. I try to remember to pray as I converse with people. It's an amazing experience to see how quickly the Lord gives me what to say and how to say it. I have never met a Christian, who is sharing his faith with those the Lord has placed in his life, who is unexcited.

An Exciting Experiment

I would like to suggest a seven-day experiment. Find a friend in Christ with whom you can share the experience. Covenant together to spend a week praying for a new awareness of what the Lord prepares. Commit yourself to make the most of every opportunity at home, at work, wherever you are. Consciously pray, "Lord, what are you up to now? What do you want in this situation? What should I say to this person?" Then at the end of the week, get together with your covenant friend to share what has happened. I promise you that you will want to make every week of the rest of your life like that!

Become What You Were Meant to Be

+ + +

Colossians 4:7-18

One of the finest compliments I ever heard was given to a friend of mine. "He's an affirmer. When I'm with him I feel good about being me. But more than that, I feel encouraged to become all that God intended me to be. It's as if he says with his whole attitude, 'Become all that you were meant to be!' "

That's the way Paul affected his friends. He had a way of liberating the best in people, and this last section of Colossians shows us how he did it. The listing of his friends is accompanied by a personal note of affirmation about each one. Some heard his dictation and others read the epistle. In either case, they were encouraged to become all that Paul believed they could be. That he felt free to mention them is in itself a great credit to them. Paul was a prisoner. To be his friend was dangerous. They could be implicated by their involvement with him. Apparently they did not care. They belonged to Christ, and in a wonderful way, to Paul and the Christian movement.

Brother-Brother Tychicus

The first to be mentioned in the hall of honor was Tychicus. The Colossians knew of him. He came from their own province of Asia. Some suggest that he was the one who brought the offering to the distressed Christians in Jerusalem referred to in Acts 20:4. Ephesians 6:21 tells that he was charged to carry the Ephesian letter to the churches. From the Colossian letter we learn a great deal about him. Paul uses three designations. Tychicus as "a dear brother, a faithful minister and fellow servant in the Lord" (Col. 4:7).

The other day I heard a Christian friend referred to as a "brother-brother." The person was reaching for a superlative expression of the quality of Christian love in the family of faith. In Christ we are given as gifts to each other for a relationship in the faith which often exceeds the filial affection of the human family. Friendship in Christ is a profound, mutual caring and concern.

I am filled with inexpressible gratitude for my brothers and sisters in Christ. The Lord has loved me richly through them. I could not do what I do without them. They bring correction when I need it, strength when I am weak, hope when I am uncertain. Hundreds of faces flash before my mind's eye. My heart fills with praise.

As If to Christ

The key to dynamic relationships in the fellowship is daring to minister to one another as if to Christ. The Christian fellowship is to be uniquely different from any other association. There is no place for competition or struggle for authority and power over one another. We are to be servants to one another, to prefer one another in love.

Critical judgments and negative put-downs are a sure sign we are out of fellowship with the Servant-Saviour. A reliable guide is to ask, "If I were to relate to this person as I would to Christ, what would I say and do?" Add to that the prayer for the Lord's guidance and power to obey, "Lord, what do you want in this person's life? How can I enable that? Help me, Jesus!"

That's in keeping with Christ's example and admonition. He was a servant among His disciples. They never forgot the way He washed their feet at the Last Supper. He asked the question which exposed their bristling competitiveness, "Do you understand what I have done for you? . . . You call me 'Teacher' and 'Lord,' and rightly so, for that is what I am. Now that I, your Lord and Teacher, have washed your feet, you also should wash one another's feet. I have set you an example that you should do as I have done for you. I tell you the truth, no servant is greater than his master, nor is a messenger greater than the one who sent him. Once you know these things, you will be blessed if you do them" (John 13:12-17).

That leaves us with the disturbing inventory of how we have washed one another's feet. It will mean very different things for each person's unique and personal needs—listening, an act of sacrificial giving, a word of assurance, a lifting of a load. The Lord will tell us, be sure of that!

Paul recognizes Tychicus as a faithful minister and fellow servant of the Lord. The words servant and slave are used in the Greek. What an affirmation for Tychicus to be recognized as Paul's fellow worker before the early church! It is implied that they ministered together, that Paul honored Tychicus' own ministry and that the fellow minister had served the Apostle's needs. Closeness, shared intimacy in the Spirit, mutual concern, involvement together in an adventure—all are indicated by Paul's image-building words: "I am sending him to you for the express purpose that you may know about our circumstances and that he may encourage your hearts" (Col. 4:8). Elevating words of esteem, indeed! How deeply the Colossians must have loved Tychicus after reading that.

A Fellowship of Reconciliation

Paul's reference to Onesimus is filled with grace. He was a runaway slave belonging to Philemon, a member of the Colossian church. Paul does not refer to him as a slave, but as a "faithful and dear brother" (4:9).

Onesimus had reached Rome in his flight and had been accepted and loved in the inclusive fellowship of the church in Paul's quarters. Obviously, he had accepted Christ as Saviour and joined the Lord's people. The New Testament letter to Philemon helps us to understand Paul's desire to have Onesimus forgiven and received not as a slave, but as an equal brother in Christ. Paul knew that neither Onesimus nor Philemon could grow in Christ without reconciliation. Onesimus had to make restitution; Philemon had to express the Lord's forgiveness.

We all have Onesimuses in our lives and we have all been an Onesimus at some time. And we can empathize with Philemon. We've been in his skin facing the challenge to forgive and forget. It's not easy to either seek forgiveness or give it. Only Christ can do either through us.

But often we need a reconciler like Paul. Note the way he intercedes for Onesimus in the letter to Philemon: "I am sending him—who is my very heart—back to you. I would have liked to keep him with me so that he could take your place in helping me while I am in chains for the gospel . . . Perhaps the reason he was separated from you for a little while was that you might have him back for good—no longer as a slave, but better than a slave, as a dear brother. He is very dear to me but even dearer to you, both as a man and as a brother in the Lord . . . welcome him as you would welcome me" (Philem. 12-17).

That's putting your life on the line! Paul not only affirmed the genuine conversion of Onesimus but expressed his love and called for the Colossians to do the same. Lightfoot comments, "The man . . . is thus commended to them as no more slave but a brother, no more dishonest and faithless but trustworthy, no more an object of contempt but of love."[1]

Paul helped Onesimus become what he now was— a new man in Christ filled with the Holy Spirit. A slave of Philemon had become a slave of Christ. Philemon and Onesimus were now *brothers!*

The Affirmation of Appreciation

Next Paul mentions Aristarchus. He's a person in the New Testament church I would like to have known personally. I'd like to be able to emulate his faithfulness and consistency. As a new Christian, Aristarchus and another disciple, Gaius, were seized by the people of Ephesus in a conflict with silversmiths over the diminished sales of silver shrines of their goddess, Artemis. The conflict was the result of the influence of the gospel preached by Paul. Aristarchus was dragged and beaten and barely escaped with his life in the riot in the theater of Ephesus (see Acts 19). He stood firm for what he believed. That conviction made him a faithful servant of Paul in the arduous trial in Jerusalem and Caesarea.

Aristarchus remained close to the Apostle throughout the treacherous sea voyage to Rome (see Acts 27:2), and obviously was incarcerated as a fellow prisoner: "My fellow prisoner Aristarchus sends you his greetings" (Col. 4:10). Paul did not allow his beloved friend's valor and constancy go without recognition. It was the Apostle's way of saying "thank you" publicly. There is affirming power in words of appreciation. Paul's heart was very tender with gratitude for his friend whose loyalty had cost him so much.

Christ's Power for New Beginnings

The mention of Mark is startling. There's rich biography behind this reference and parenthetical instruction to the Colossians about him which illustrates Christ's power in the lives of His people.

This is John Mark whose home in Jerusalem offered a "large upper room" where Jesus celebrated the Passover and the Last Supper (see Luke 22:7-13). That same Upper Room became the site of the birth of the Church at Pentecost and the headquarters of the apostles, afterward.

Mark had been a part of the exciting events as the infant church grew. He was persecuted by Saul of Tarsus and was among those scattered abroad under the purge of the Sanhedrin. After Paul's conversion, Mark's life was strangely intertwined with the Apostle's (see Acts 12:25). But the strong ties were broken when Mark defected at Perga (Acts 13:13). It took the encouraging ministry of his cousin Barnabas to nurse him back to spiritual health after that deflating failure (Acts 15:37-39). Mark then came under the influence of Peter who helped him grow up in Christ (1 Pet. 5:13). The "failure" became a great man of faith and authored the first Gospel to be written, utilizing the firsthand witness of Peter.

But it took years for his broken relationship with Paul to be healed. How realistic and honest the Scriptures are! Those pioneers of the faith had the same problems we have today. Paul was the initiator of the reconciliation. He called for the man he had refused to take on the second missionary journey. The Apostle not only wanted to straighten things out, but he wanted Mark to be with him. Gracious maturity!

Now Paul wanted the Colossians to accept the remade Mark as a brother. He wanted them to think of him not as a defector but as a defender of the faith. Surely Mark overheard these reaffirming remarks. It encouraged him to be fully the man Paul claimed him to be.

The mention of Mark challenges us to think of the people we have written off or hope we never see again. The other day I overheard a great Christian leader say about another leader, "If I never see that guy again it will be too soon." I was shocked and then a bit judgmental of my respected friend. Then I was forced to think of people in my own life I had neglected or with whom I had refused to initiate reconciliation. I had such good reasons! But none of them impressed the Lord. We all have some John Marks to call for and affirm as fellow strugglers who need our warmth and chance for a new beginning.

Ushered into Glory

Paul makes reference to a "Jesus who was called Justus" (Col. 4:11). He is an unknown disciple. We know nothing about him other than what we can glean from his name. "Jesus" was a common Hebrew name, a transliteration of the name *Joshua* or *Jehoshua*. The surname Justus was a familiar designation of Jews who were of the circumcision and devoted to the Law. Here Paul's use of his full name indicates emphasis on the fact that he was a converted Hebrew.

The most important thing, however, was that Jesus Justus was mentioned at all. He must have been a special help and comfort to the Apostle. His faithfulness to Christ, in spite of the rejection of the hostile Jews in Rome and the danger of arrest for complicity with a Roman prisoner, earned him a place in Paul's heart and a line in sacred Scripture.

We never know the results of being obedient to Christ and the fellowship. Jesus Justus was ushered into glory he had never sought, but justly deserved.

His name has been read for centuries in memory of an unknown disciple who was distinguished for his dedication to the church at Rome and to Paul.

A Prayer Wrestler

Epaphras has already been mentioned by Paul in the opening of the letter. He was the contagious evangelist who had founded the Colossian church. Paul tells the Colossians that "he is always wrestling in prayer for you" (4:12). There are few finer things which could be said about a person.

Thank God for the tireless prayer warriors who intercede for us! It is frightening to imagine what life would be like without them. I could not minister, preach with any power, or be effective in introducing people to Christ if there were not hundreds of Epaphrases praying for me.

We can learn how to pray from this saint, Epaphras. Note the content of his prayers. He was praying that the Colossian Christians would "stand firm in all the will of God, mature and fully assured" (4: 12). Quite a prayer! He longed for his children in the faith to know the full dimensions of the will of God for all of life. He knew of the excruciating pressures on them to compromise or syncretize the gospel with Gnosticism. When he prayed that they become "mature and fully assured," he was responding to the very heart of God. The Lord wanted that for the Colossians. Epaphras had learned how to cooperate with God by praying for the very thing God wanted most to give the evangelist's friends.

By praising Epaphras' prayer, Paul was also encouraging the Colossians by helping them to know that the Church as a whole knew of their struggle and was praying for them. The reference to how hard Epaphras was working for them gave them a sense of their importance and value. It must have brought joy to Epaphras to have the Apostle recognize his conscientiousness.

The Beloved Physician

"Our dear friend Luke, the doctor ... " (4:14). Paul and Luke had been through a great deal since the Lord had brought them together at Troas years before (implied in Acts 16:10 when author Luke begins using pronoun "we"). From the time they set out for Macedonia together, Luke had not left the Apostle's side, Praise God for that! Not only was Paul encouraged and inspired by the physician's intellectual and spiritual depth, but as a result of Luke's companionship with Paul we have the Gospel of Luke and the Acts of the Apostles.

The Holy Spirit-filled and empowered adventurer for the Lord was concerned about the Colossians though he had never met them. The amazing thing about the reference to his name here at the end of the Colossian letter was the bond of intertwining love which bound all of these people together whether they had ever met or not. Luke was concerned about the Colossians as if he had founded the church himself.

The Affirmation of Silence

Demas, his name a contraction of Demetrius, is mentioned in passing. If we leaf over to 2 Timothy 4:10 we find the reason. Second Timothy was written during Paul's second imprisonment in Rome, some time after the first imprisonment during which he wrote Colossians. Paul was awaiting execution. A pathetic note of disappointment was attached to his reference to Demas in the second letter to Timothy: "Demas, because he loved this world, has deserted me and has gone to Thessalonica." It was too dangerous for him in Rome. Demas left the Apostle when he most needed him. He was afraid for his life. He loved this world too much.

The lack of any descriptive words about Demas in the Colossian letter suggests that the seeds of defection and desertion were already planted in him and Paul sensed the instability in the wavering disciple. The Apostle's lack of verbal affirmation was in itself a compassionate expression of love for Demas. He did not tell the Colossians about what he suspected was happening. This, at least, is my supposition about why Demas was mentioned, but not with any words of approbation.

The House-Church in Laodicea

As Paul draws his dictation of the Colossian letter to a close, his mind leaps up the river 12 miles to the city of Laodicea. The two cities were almost one in the Apostle's mind as he thought of the Christians in the Lycus Valley of the province of Asia. His concern is specifically expressed for the church in Laodicea which met in the house of Nympha, a woman leader and hostess of the fellowship. The words, "church in her house" (Col. 4:15), ring with meaning. There were no church buildings then. The church met in houses. It is significant that in our time some of the most vital churches in miniature are meeting in neighborhood Bible study and prayer groups and house-churches. These small, intimate, caring fellowships of God's people are surging new life into large, institutional churches. The pattern is scriptural as we can see from this passage.

Paul's concern for the Laodicean Christians was justified. It was not any easier to be a Christian in the prosperous, wealthy city than in philosophically confused Colosse. Not many years passed before the Lord Himself spoke a word of judgment through the apostle John on Patmos: "I know your deeds, that you are neither cold nor hot. I wish you were either one or the other! So, because you are lukewarm—neither hot nor cold—I am about to spit you out of my mouth" (Rev. 3:15,16).

But the word of chastisement was followed by hope: "Those whom I love I rebuke and discipline. So be earnest, and repent. Here I am! I stand at the door and knock. If anyone hears my voice and opens the door, I will go in and eat with him, and he with me" (Rev. 3:19,20).

Paul had anticipated the Lord's judgment in his anxiety about the Colossians' neighbors who thought they were rich when they were poor spiritually. What a heart the Apostle had!

Archippus in the Colossian church is reminded of an assignment Paul had given him. The reassignment is direct and imperious: "See to it that you complete the work you have received in the Lord" (Col. 4:17). Accountability is a part of discipleship. Sloppy work that hits wide of the Lord's goals is not condoned. Archippus is to discharge his task fully, *pleroo*, to "fulfill it completely." Love is expressed in recognizing the Christian worker, honoring his task and encouraging his best. Paul had a quality of tough love.

The Affirmation of a Personal Word

Paul finishes the letter in his own hand. He takes the dictated portion from the scribe and writes the final sentence himself. His hands are in chains. With love and urgency he writes: "I, Paul, write this greeting in my own hand. Remember my chains. Grace be with you" (4:18). He was in the bond of the chains, but his heart was bonded to the Colossians with the chains of love.

The last words capsulize the whole letter, and are more than a traditional ending to a letter. Grace was the essence of the Apostle's message. The Lord's unchanging, cross-oriented love was Paul's deepest passion and the Colossians' greatest need.

Our study of Colossians has been a fresh experience of the grace of the Lord Jesus for me. The sublime and supreme adequacy of Christ is all that I need to know. The secret of power is to give all that we know of ourselves to all that we know of Christ. Colossians has helped me to know more of both, and I am thankful.

Footnote

1. Lightfoot, *Commentary on St. Paul's Epistle to the Colossians and Philemon*, p. 233.